MW00353845

GLOBETROTTER
TRAVEL ATLAS

Road Atlas of
ZIMBABWE

NH
NEW HOLLAND

Published in 1995 by
New Holland (Publishers) Ltd
London • Cape Town • Sydney

ISBN 1 85368 518 6

New Holland (Publishers) Ltd
Chapel House, 24 Nutford Place,
London W1H 6DQ

Project Manager: Simon Atkinson
Text: Paul Tingay
Editor: Peter Joyce
Design Concept: Neville Poulter
Designer: Lyndall Hamilton
Concept and Cartographer: John Hall
DTP Maps: John Loubser
Researcher: Estelle Cohen
Reproduction by Hirt & Carter (Pty) Ltd,
Cape Town
Printed and Bound in Singapore by
Tien Wah Press (Pte) Ltd

Photographic Credits
Daryl Balfour: page 25 top right; **Colin
Bell:** pages 34 top, 42 top, 61 bottom right;
Tom Bulpin: page 32 top; **Gerald Cubitt:**
title, page 8 left and right, 9 bottom right,
16 top left and right, 26 bottom right, 28
top right, 30 bottom, 32 bottom, 34 bottom left and right, 37 above and below, 42
bottom, 44 top, 48 right, 54 top, 56 top
and bottom, 61 bottom left; **Dook:** page 18
top right; **Milton Evangelou:** pages 18 top
left; **Roger de la Harpe:** pages 20 top, 33
top; **Colin Paterson-Jones:** page 51 bottom; **Jan Teede:** pages 18 bottom, 20 bottom right, 54 bottom right; **Mark van
Aardt:** Cover, pages 4, 9 bottom left, 13
middle, 20 bottom left, 21 bottom, 26 top,
28 top left and bottom, 30 top, 48 left;
Friedrich von Hörsten: pages 9 top right,
13 top and bottom, 16 bottom right, 24
right, 25 top left and bottom, 35 top, 44
bottom, 51 top, 54 bottom left, 61 top;
Peter Pickford: pages 20 bottom right [SIL],
21 top [SIL], 26 bottom left [SIL]; **Brendan
Ryan** page 6 [ABPL]; **Lanz von Hörsten:**
page 24 top; **Patrick Wagner:** pages 9 top
left [PHOTO ACCESS].

Distance Chart

BEITBRIDGE	BINDURA	BULAWAYO	CHIMANIMANI	CHINHOYI	CHIPINGA	CHIREDZI	CHIRUNDU	CHIVHU	FRANCISTOWN	GWANDA	GWERU	HARARE	HWANGE	KADOMA	KARIBA	KWEKWE	MARONDERA	MASVINGO	MHANGURA	MUTARE	MVUMA	MVURWI	NYAMAPANDA	NYANGA	PLUMTREE	RUSAPE	VICTORIA FALLS	ZVISHAVANE	APPROXIMATE DISTANCE IN KILOMETRES
	670	320	545	695	505	300	930	440	510	195	470	580	655	605	950	535	655	290	765	585	390	680	825	690	420	680	760	380	BEITBRIDGE
670		525	500	205	530	580	440	230	715	660	360	90	860	230	460	300	165	380	220	350	280	110	335	360	625	260	965	475	BINDURA
320	525		565	430	520	485	660	300	190	125	165	440	335	300	680	225	510	285	500	580	245	525	680	685	100	610	440	190	BULAWAYO
545	500	565		530	70	255	765	430	750	560	460	415	900	555	780	520	340	280	600	150	380	515	660	255	665	245	1000	375	CHIMANIMANI
695	205	430	530		555	605	235	255	615	580	260	115	760	130	255	200	190	405	70	380	310	100	360	385	525	285	865	400	CHINHOYI
505	530	520	70	555		210	790	385	710	515	420	440	855	550	810	480	365	235	625	175	335	540	725	280	620	270	960	335	CHIPINGA
300	580	485	255	605	210		840	350	670	480	380	490	820	515	860	440	505	200	675	315	300	590	735	420	585	410	920	295	CHIREDZI
930	440	660	765	235	790	840		490	850	815	500	350	995	365	135	435	425	640	260	615	545	390	600	620	760	520	1100	635	CHIRUNDU
440	230	300	430	255	385	350	490		485	430	135	140	630	265	510	195	215	150	325	400	50	240	385	410	395	310	735	245	CHIVHU
510	715	190	750	615	710	670	850	485		315	350	625	520	485	865	415	700	470	685	770	435	715	870	870	85	795	625	375	FRANCISTOWN
195	660	125	560	580	515	480	815	430	315		320	570	460	450	835	380	645	280	650	575	375	670	815	680	225	670	565	180	GWANDA
470	360	165	460	260	420	380	500	135	350	320		275	500	135	515	60	350	180	335	480	80	375	520	540	265	445	600	135	GWERU
580	90	440	415	115	440	490	350	140	625	570	275		770	140	370	210	75	290	185	265	190	100	245	270	540	170	875	390	HARARE
655	860	335	900	760	855	820	995	630	520	460	500	770		630	1015	560	845	620	830	915	580	875	1015	1020	435	1000	105	520	HWANGE
605	230	300	555	130	550	515	365	265	485	450	135	140	630		380	70	215	315	200	405	145	245	385	410	400	310	735	270	KADOMA
950	460	680	780	255	810	860	135	510	865	835	515	370	1015	380		355	445	660	275	630	560	350	615	640	780	540	1120	650	KARIBA
535	300	225	520	200	480	440	435	195	415	380	60	210	560	70	355		290	245	270	475	145	315	460	480	325	385	665	200	KWEKWE
655	165	510	340	190	365	505	425	215	700	645	350	75	845	215	445	290		365	260	190	265	175	320	195	610	95	950	460	MARONDERA
290	380	285	280	405	235	200	640	150	470	280	180	290	620	315	660	245	365		480	295	100	390	535	400	385	390	725	100	MASVINGO
765	220	500	600	70	625	675	260	325	685	650	335	185	830	200	275	270	260	480		450	455	110	430	455	600	360	935	470	MHANGURA
585	350	580	150	380	175	315	615	400	770	575	480	265	915	405	630	475	190	295	450		395	365	510	100	680	95	1020	395	MUTARE
390	280	245	380	310	335	300	545	50	435	375	80	190	580	145	560	145	265	100	455	395		295	435	500	345	490	685	200	MVUMA
680	110	525	515	100	540	590	390	240	715	670	375	100	875	245	350	315	175	390	110	365	295		350	370	625	270	965	490	MVURWI
825	335	680	660	360	725	735	600	385	870	815	520	245	1015	385	615	460	320	535	430	510	435	350		515	780	415	1120	630	NYAMAPANDA
690	360	685	255	385	280	420	620	410	870	680	540	270	1020	410	640	480	195	400	455	100	500	370	515		785	100	1145	495	NYANGA
420	625	100	665	525	620	585	760	395	85	225	265	540	435	400	780	325	610	385	600	680	345	625	780	785		705	540	290	PLUMTREE
680	260	610	245	285	270	410	520	310	795	670	445	170	1000	310	540	385	95	390	360	95	490	270	415	100	705		1045	485	RUSAPE
760	965	440	1000	865	960	920	1100	735	625	565	600	875	105	735	1120	665	950	725	935	1020	685	965	1120	1145	540	1045		625	VICTORIA FALLS
380	475	190	375	400	335	295	635	245	375	180	135	390	520	270	650	200	460	100	470	395	200	490	630	495	290	485	625		ZVISHAVANE

Town Plan Legend

Main roads & malls	Haupt und Einkaufsstraßen / Route principale et Mall — MALL
Roads	Straßen / Route
Railways	Eisenbahn / Ligne de chemin de fer
Parks & sports fields	Parks und Sportplätze / Parc et terrain de sports
Hospitals	Krankenhaus / Hôpital — ✚
Caravan parks	Wohnwagenpark / Camping-caravaning
Hotels	Hotel / Hôtel — JAMESON (H)
Bus terminus	Endstation / Terminus bus
Buildings of interest	Wichtige Bauwerke / Monument à voir
Places of interest	Sehenswürdigkeiten / Endroit à voir — ● Ruins
Places of worship	Gotteshaus / Lieu du culte — △
Police stations	Polizeirevier / Poste de police — ●
Parking areas	Parkplatz / Parking — P
Post offices	Post / Bureau de poste — ✉
Library	Bibliothek / Bibliothèque
Ferries	Fähre / Ferry/bac — F
Information	Auskunftsbüro / Centre d'information — i
Built-up areas	Wohngebiet / Agglomération
One-way streets	Einbahnstraße / Rue à sens-unique — →
Major petrol stops	Große Tankstelle / Station-service

Contents

Key Tourist Areas

Main Map Section

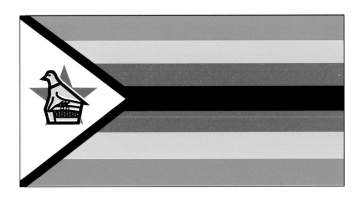

Zimbabwe was born at midnight on 18 April 1980. Its new flag featured the colour bands of green, gold, red and black which represent, respectively, the land, mineral wealth, the bloodshed caused by the fight for freedom, and the country's people. Also on the flag is the Zimbabwe bird, an important emblem in the country's history.

National Route Planner

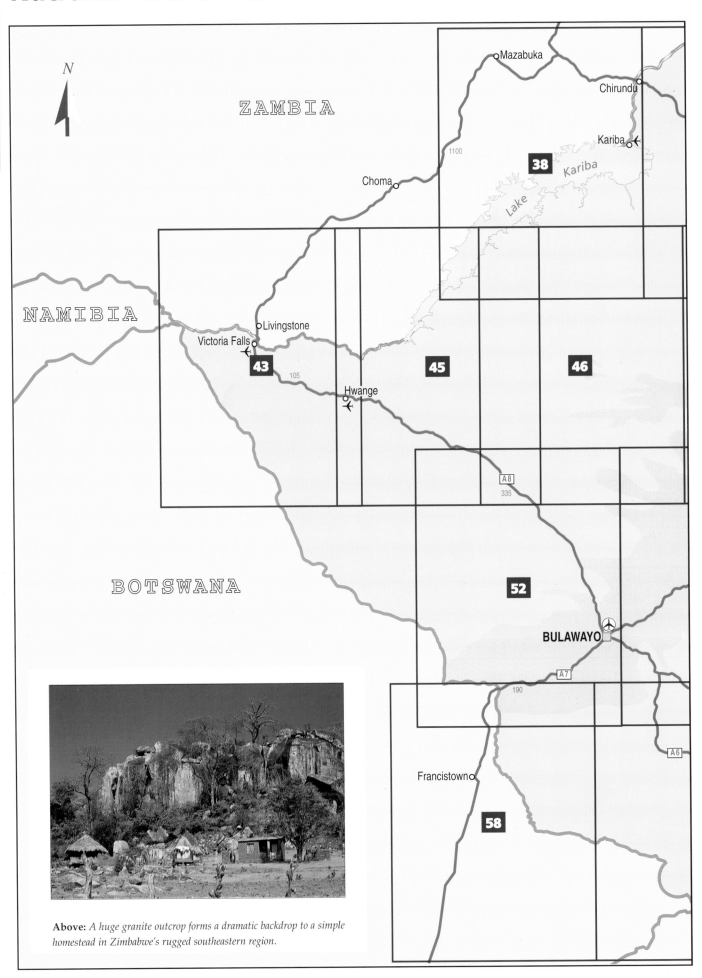

N

ZAMBIA

Mazabuka

Chirundu

Kariba

38

Kariba

Lake

Choma

1100

NAMIBIA

Livingstone

Victoria Falls

43

105

45

46

Hwange

A8

335

BOTSWANA

52

BULAWAYO

A7

190

A6

Francistown

58

Above: *A huge granite outcrop forms a dramatic backdrop to a simple homestead in Zimbabwe's rugged southeastern region.*

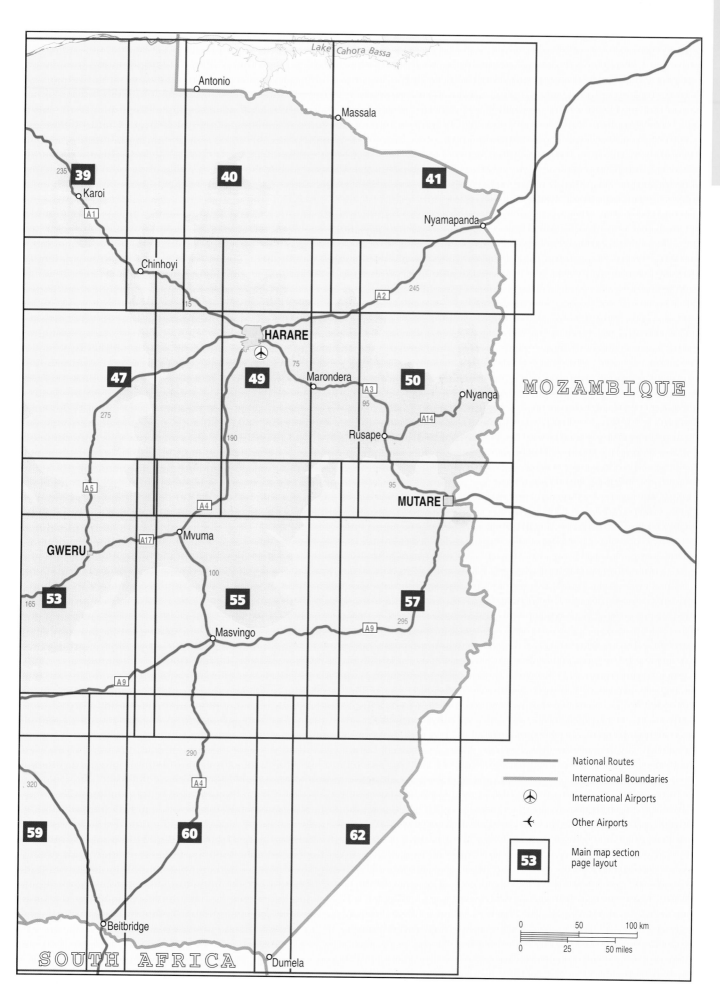

Antonio

Lake Cahora Bassa

Massala

235 **39** Karoi

A1

40

41

Nyamapanda

Chinhoyi

A2 245

15

HARARE

47

49 Marondera

50

A3

Nyanga

95

Rusape

275

A14

190

MOZAMBIQUE

95

A5

MUTARE

A4

GWERU

Mvuma

A17

100

165 **53**

55

57

Masvingo

A9 295

A9

290

A4

59

60

62

Beitbridge

SOUTH AFRICA

Dumela

National Routes

International Boundaries

International Airports

Other Airports

53 Main map section page layout

0 50 100 km

0 25 50 miles

5

Key Tourist Areas

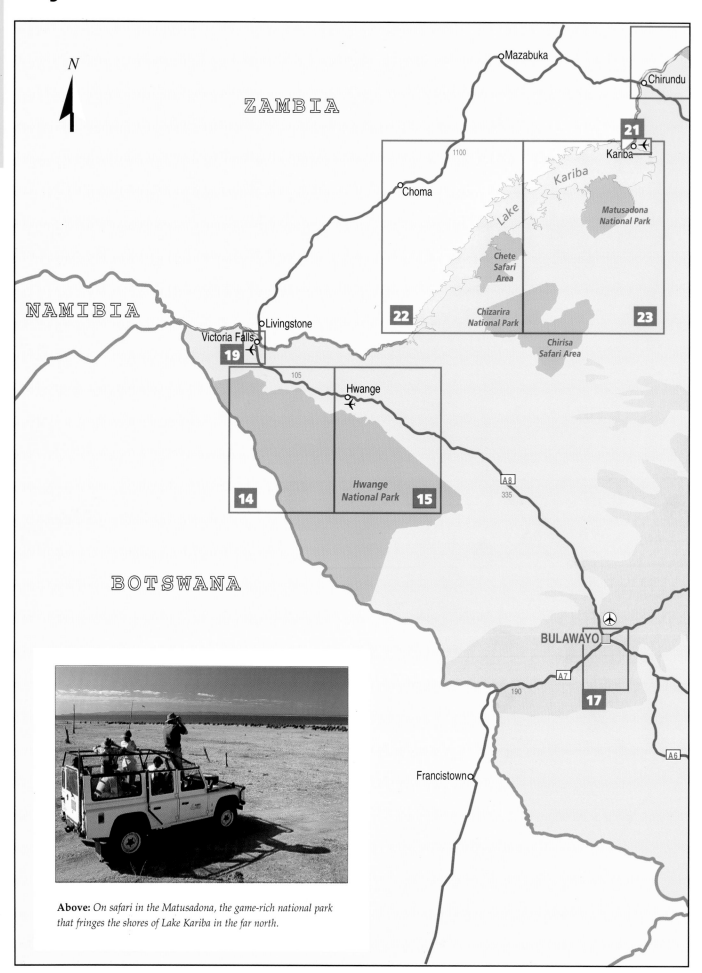

ZAMBIA

Mazabuka

Chirundu

21

Choma

1100

Kariba

Lake Kariba

Matusadona
National Park

NAMIBIA

Livingstone

22

Chete
Safari
Area

Chizarira
National Park

23

Victoria Falls

19

Chirisa
Safari
Area

105

Hwange

14

Hwange
National Park

15

A8

335

BOTSWANA

BULAWAYO

17

A7

190

A6

Francistown

Above: *On safari in the Matusadona, the game-rich national park*
that fringes the shores of Lake Kariba in the far north.

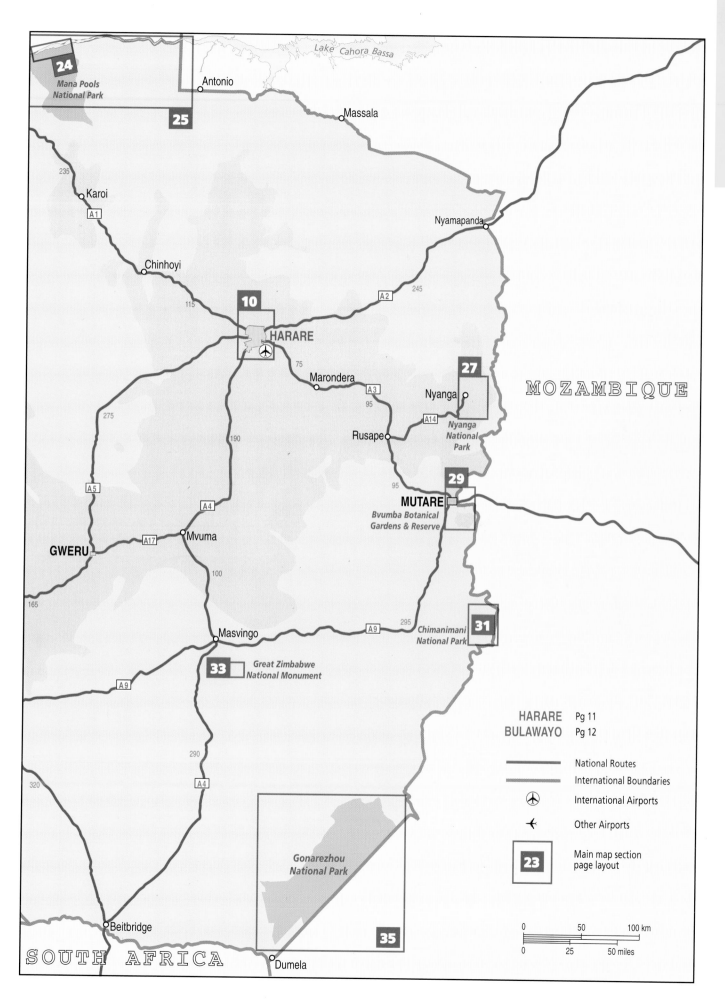

24 Mana Pools National Park

Lake Cahora Bassa

Antonio

Massala

25

235

Karoi

A1

Chinhoyi

115

10 HARARE

75

Marondera

A3

A2 245

Nyamapanda

MOZAMBIQUE

27

Nyanga

A14

95

Rusape

Nyanga National Park

95

29

MUTARE

Bvumba Botanical Gardens & Reserve

275

190

A5

A4

A17

GWERU

Mvuma

100

165

Masvingo

295 **31**

A9

Chimanimani National Park

33 *Great Zimbabwe National Monument*

A9

290

A4

320

35

Gonarezhou National Park

Beitbridge

SOUTH AFRICA

Dumela

HARARE   Pg 11
BULAWAYO Pg 12

National Routes

International Boundaries

✈ International Airports

✈ Other Airports

23 Main map section page layout

0   50   100 km

0   25   50 miles

7

Key Tourist Areas Legend

National roads / Nationalrouten / Route nationale	Border posts / Grenzübergang / Poste de contrôle	Buildings of interest / Wichtige Bauwerke / Monument à voir
Principal roads / Nationalstraßen / Route de liaison régionale	Scenic routes / Malerische Landschaft / Route panoramique	Major petrol stops / Große Tankstelle / Station-service
Main roads / Hauptstraßen / Route principale	Mountain passes / Bergpässe / Col	Hotels (selected) / Hotel (Auswahl) / Hôtel
Minor roads / Nebenstraßen / Route secondaire	Game & nature reserves / Wild und Naturschutzgebiete / Réserve naturelle	Camps / Ferienlager / Camp
Tracks / Sandweg / Piste	Mountain ranges / Gebirge / Chaîne de montagnes	Caravan parks / Wohwagenpark / Camping-caravaning
Footpath / Wanderwege / Circuit de randonnée	Airports / Flughäfen / Aéroport	Places of interest / Sehenswürdigkeiten / Endroit à voir
Route numbers / Routenummern / Numéro de route	Cities / Großstadt / Grande ville	Stations (selected) / Bahnhof (Auswahl) / Gare
Distances / Entfernungen / Distance	Towns / Stadt / Ville secondaire	Area names / Gebiet / Nom de la région
Railways / Eisenbahn / Chemin de fer	Small towns / Kleinstadt / Petite ville	Peaks in metres / Höhe in Metern / Sommet
International boundary / Landesgrenzen / Frontière internationale	Villages / Dorf / Petit village	Water features / Gewässer / Hydrographie

Border posts example: Chirundu

Mountain passes example: Moodies

Game & nature reserves example: Hwange N.P.

Mountain ranges example: WEDZA

Airports: INT. / Other

Places of interest example: Ruins

Area names example: Matobo

Peaks in metres example: Dombo 2005m ▲

Water features example: River / Dam / Swamp

Left: *Traditional dancing at the Chapungu Kraal on the eastern edge of Harare.*
Above: *The delicate flame lily, Gloriosa superba, whose colours vary from blood-red to bright yellow. A diamond brooch in the shape of the flower was presented to Princess (now Queen) Elizabeth during the 1947 Royal visit, after which it was adopted as one of the country's national emblems.*

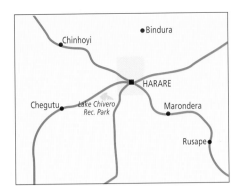

Harare and Surrounds

Zimbabwe's capital, Harare, set some 1470m (4823ft) above sea level on the highveld ridge, is a small city by international standards, though the wider metropolitan area embraces a population of more than a million. Its central business district is a modern, bustling complex of neat-looking buildings and unusually broad thoroughfares that conform to a strict grid; its outlying avenues, notably those to the north, are graced by a myriad flowering trees. The suburbs are particularly lovely in springtime, when the jacarandas display their feathery, lilac-coloured blooms, but other tree species are almost as numerous and beautiful.

Of special note are Harare's public gardens, a stone's throw from the city centre and a delightfully refreshing oasis of lawns, exotic and indigenous trees, trimmed beddings, a bandstand and open-air theatre.

On their southern perimeter stands the architecturally striking National Gallery, repository of, among other things, some splendid Zimbabwean stone sculpture – a distinctive art form that has earned wide acclaim. According to the experts, at least five of the world's leading sculptor-carvers are Zimbabwean. Fine examples, too, can be seen in the Vhukutiwa Garden in Milton Park, and in the Chapungu Kraal, a recreated Shona village on the eastern edge of the city. The latter also features African tribal and traditional dancing at weekends, accompanied by a live *marimba* band.

There is a sculpture of a quite different kind at Heroe's Acre, a 57ha (141 acre) monument to those who fell during the guerrilla war that finally ended with independence in 1980. Principal elements here are the bronze statue of the Unknown Soldier, and a site museum that tells the story of that grim conflict.

A must for visitors in search of local colour is Musika Market in the 'tin and mango' suburb and bus terminus of Mbare, to the south of the city – a crowded, noisy, wonderfully vital place offering crafts, fruit,

vegetables, herbal potions and much else. Situated in Willowvale is a more sedate but equally fascinating emporium, the Tobacco Sales Floor – the largest tobacco auction centre in the world. Visitors are welcome to listen to the frantic bidding and tour the floors from April through to October.

Nature lovers have plenty to choose from in and around Harare. Among the drawcards are the Mukuvisi Woodlands and game park where you can see elephant, zebra, crocodile, antelope and waterfowl. For the serious bird-watcher there are the Larvon Bird Gardens, on the Bulawayo road, which contain 250 species in walk-through aviaries.

The entrancing Ewanrigg Botanical Gardens to the northeast of Harare are famed for their aloes, and, 37km (23 miles) west of the city, is the capital's weekend playground, Lake Chivero Recreational Park, a pleasant venue for boating, sailing, fishing, game-viewing, (rhino, giraffe, zebra, buck), walking, and relaxing around a barbecue fire.

Above left: *The capital city, Harare, at night.*
Above right: *A Mashona basket-maker displays her intricate wickerwork.*
Below left: *One of the many striking 'balancing rocks' to be seen in the countryside around Harare.*
Below: *The tobacco auctions, held in Harare's Willowvale area, yield millions in foreign earnings.*

HARARE	J	F	M	A	M	J	J	A	S	O	N	D
AVERAGE TEMP. °F	70	70	68	66	61	57	57	61	66	72	72	70
AVERAGE TEMP. °C	21	21	20	19	16	14	14	16	19	22	22	21
Hours of Sun Daily	7	6	7	8	8	9	9	10	10	9	7	6
RAINFALL ins.	8	8	4	1.5	0.5	0	0	0	0	1.5	4	8
RAINFALL mm	192	181	98	42	10	4	2	3	9	38	94	194
Days of Rainfall	17	15	11	6	2	1	1	1	1	5	11	16

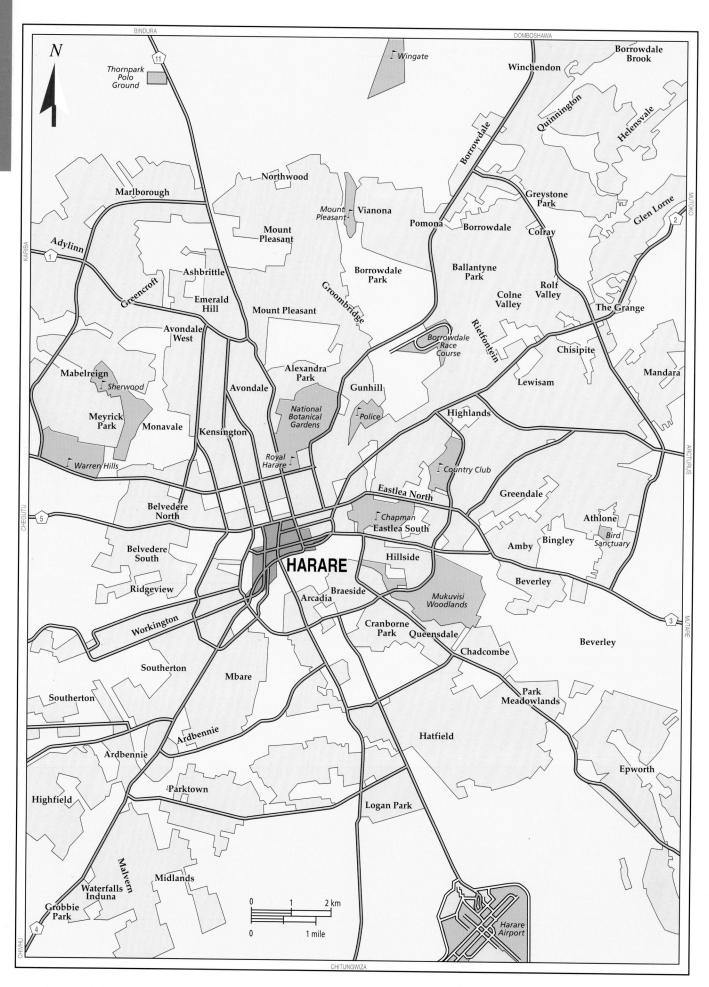

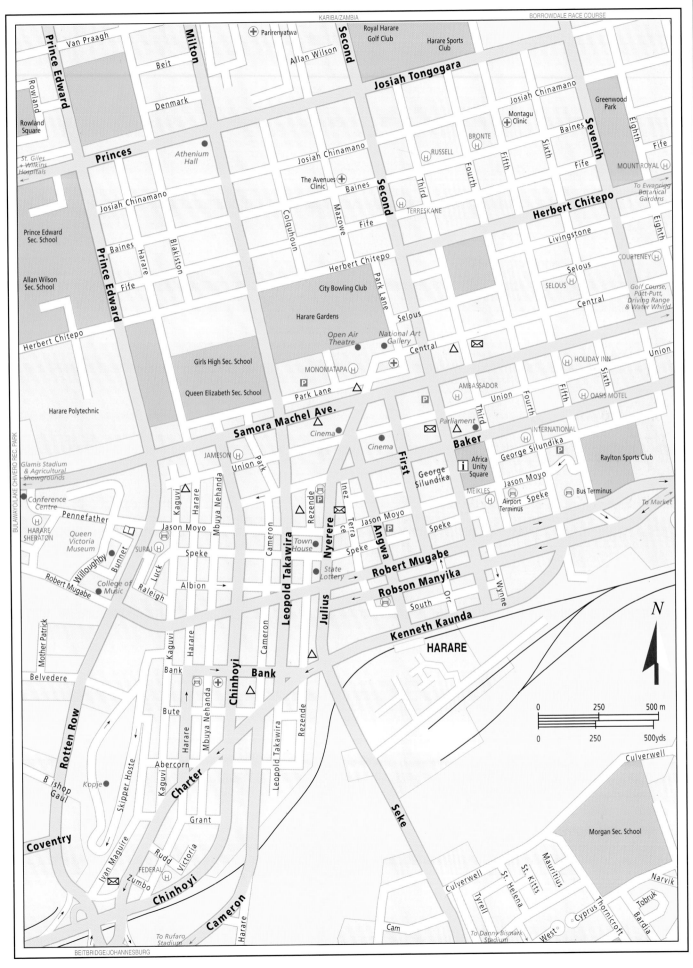

Bulawayo

Zimbabwe's second city, Bulawayo, lies at a much lower altitude and is generally hotter and drier than Harare. For much of the time the place tends to look parched, its streets covered by a thin film of Kalahari sand, but the well-watered central area and its adjacent parkland – a broad 'green lung' that flanks the Amatsheumhlope River – remains gloriously verdant throughout the year. The residential gardens, too, are lovely, and the wide thoroughfares, originally designed to allow a full span of oxen to turn, are lined by old British colonial buildings and a gorgeous profusion of jacarandas and crimson flames.

Inviting an hour's stroll is Bulawayo's Central Park, decorated by a magnificent variety of tall trees and an exquisite rose garden; and adjacent Centenary Park, a shady expanse of lawns, flowering shrubs, aviary, game enclosure and, on the perimeter, the Natural History Museum.

The museum boasts the southern hemisphere's most extensive animal collection (75,000 exhibits), the world's second largest mounted elephant, a recreated mine including a display of gold and emeralds, and the fascinating Hall of Man.

Well worth visiting, too, is the open-air vintage train museum, the earliest of whose steam locomotives first took to the tracks over a hundred years ago.

Passenger steam trains still do honourable duty on Zimbabwe's rail network, operating under the aegis of a company called Rail Safaris. A truly memorable run is the Zambezi Special rail safari: elegant 1920s coaches afford luxurious game-viewing as the train skirts the Hwange National Park on its way to the Victoria Falls (*see page 18*).

Animal lovers are welcome at the Tshabalala Game Sanctuary, where visitors can walk, ride and picnic as well as watch wildlife such as zebra, giraffe and kudu.

Those in search of local arts and crafts should make a point of visiting the Mzilikazi Art and Craft centre, in the suburb of the same name, northwest of the city centre, where potters, painters, sculptors and other craftsmen display their considerable, and in some cases internationally renowned, talent.

Recommended excursions farther afield include those to the Matobo Hills and the national park that they encompass (*see page 16*), and to the walled terraces of the Kame Ruins, the remains of a city-state established in the 17th century. Situated to the west of Bulawayo, the ruins, second in size only to Great Zimbabwe (*see page 32*), are a proclaimed World Heritage Site.

BULAWAYO	J	F	M	A	M	J	J	A	S	O	N	D
AVERAGE TEMP. °F	72	72	70	66	63	57	57	63	68	72	72	72
AVERAGE TEMP. °C	22	22	21	19	17	14	14	17	20	22	22	22
Hours of Sun Daily	7	7	8	8	9	9	9	10	9	9	7	7
RAINFALL ins.	5	4	2	1.5	0	0	0	0	0	1.5	4	5
RAINFALL mm	134	104	52	38	8	2	1	2	8	35	96	128
Days of Rainfall	12	11	4	4	2	1	1	1	1	5	10	13

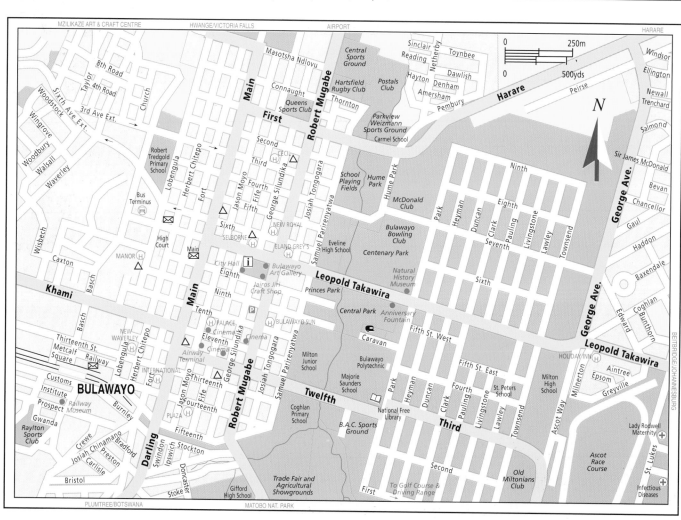

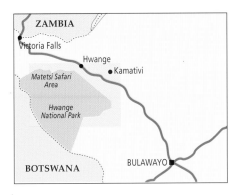

Hwange National Park

Hwange National Park, a vast, wedge-shaped expanse of rugged, heat-blistered terrain in the far west of the country, ranks among the aristocrats of Africa's game sanctuaries. It covers nearly 14,620km² (5645 sq miles) of dry Kalahari sandveld – mainly grassland plain with scattered bush and trees – and it sustains a greater variety and density of large animals than any other conservation area in the country. Specifically, Hwange is home to around 15,000 buffalo, 3000 giraffe, 3000 zebra, 16 species of antelope, including 5000 handsome kudu and 2000 sable, and an impressive 25 different kinds of carnivore.

Hwange National Park is especially known, though, for its elephants. During the rains, which in good years fall from November through to February, the herds are dispersed, many of them migrating across the border into Botswana's Chobe, Linyanti and Moremi areas. But in the dry winter season more than 20,000 of these gentle, but environmentally destructive, giants are drawn to Hwange's sixty-odd natural pans and pump-supplied waterholes.

Among the predators in the park are lion and leopard, the beautiful cheetah, and the spotted hyena and wild dog. Birdlife is prolific and around 400 species have been identified, notable among which are the raptors.

Visitors have a choice of three major camps located in the northern sector and a number of smaller campsites and lodges, all linked by around 480km (298 miles) of dirt roads along which there are picnic sites, and waterholes overlooked by viewpoints.

Main Camp is the principal entry point for the park and serves as the administrative headquarters. It has a shop, petrol station, restaurant and a variety of fully equipped cottages. A short distance from the camp is the Nyamandhlovu Pan viewing platform – an ideal vantage point for seeing a variety of wildlife, including elephant, giraffe, wildebeest, impala and buffalo.

Sinamatella Camp situated to the north-west overlooks sweeping plains famous for their elephant, and offers accommodation in luxury two-bedroomed cottages. Robins and Nantwich lie farther west in prime lion, hyena

HWANGE	J	F	M	A	M	J	J	A	S	O	N	D
AVERAGE TEMP. °F	75	73	73	70	63	57	59	63	72	75	77	75
AVERAGE TEMP. °C	24	23	23	2	17	14	15	17	22	24	25	24
Hours of Sun Daily	8	8	8	9	9	9	10	11	11	9	9	7
RAINFALL ins.	6	5	3	1.5	0	0	0	0	0	1	2	6
RAINFALL mm	162	147	72	32	4	1	0	1	4	24	67	155
Days of Rainfall	16	14	9	4	1	0	0	0	1	4	10	15

and cheetah country. Robins has game-viewing hides at Big Toms and Little Toms, situated on a tributary of the Deka River. To the east of the camp is a fossil forest and Manzinchesa hot springs.

The northern parts of the park are characterized by rocky outcrops, extensive teak forests and mopane woodlands, but the remainder of Hwange – about 80% of the park – is fairly flat and open, which is ideal

for game-viewing but which, in the interests of conservation, is accessible only to specialist or private camping and photographic safaris.

Top: *A number of Hwange's 20,000 elephant crowd around one of the park's 60 waterholes.*
Above: *Main Camp, focal point of the Hwange park. Here visitors can view wildlife by moonlight.*
Left: *Close to Main Camp is the often crowded but invariably rewarding Nyamandhlovu Pan viewing platform.*

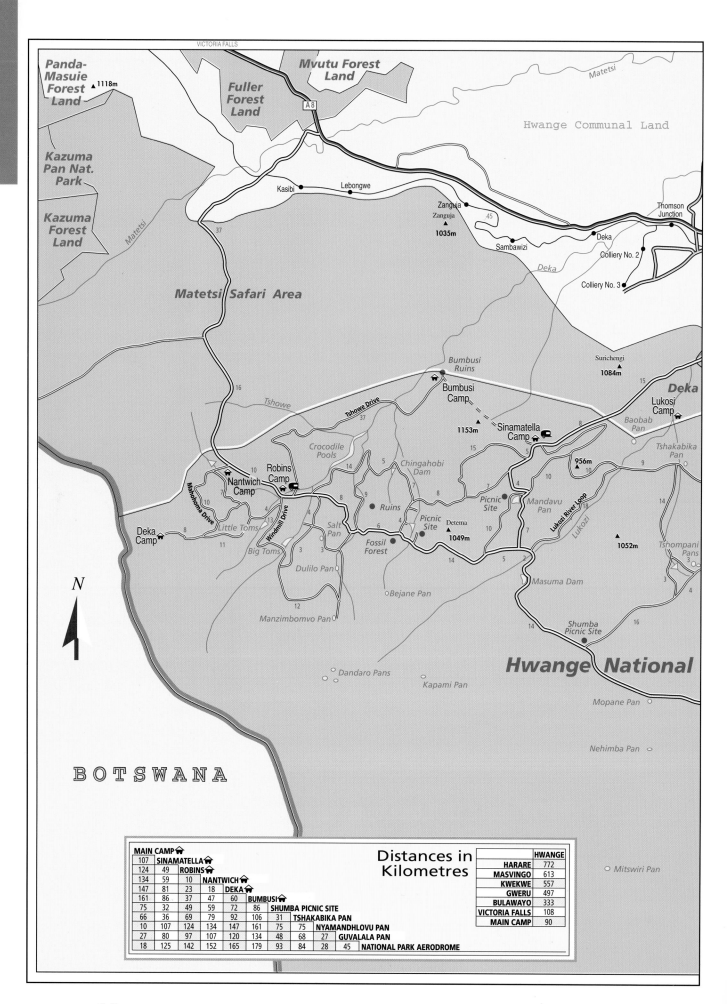

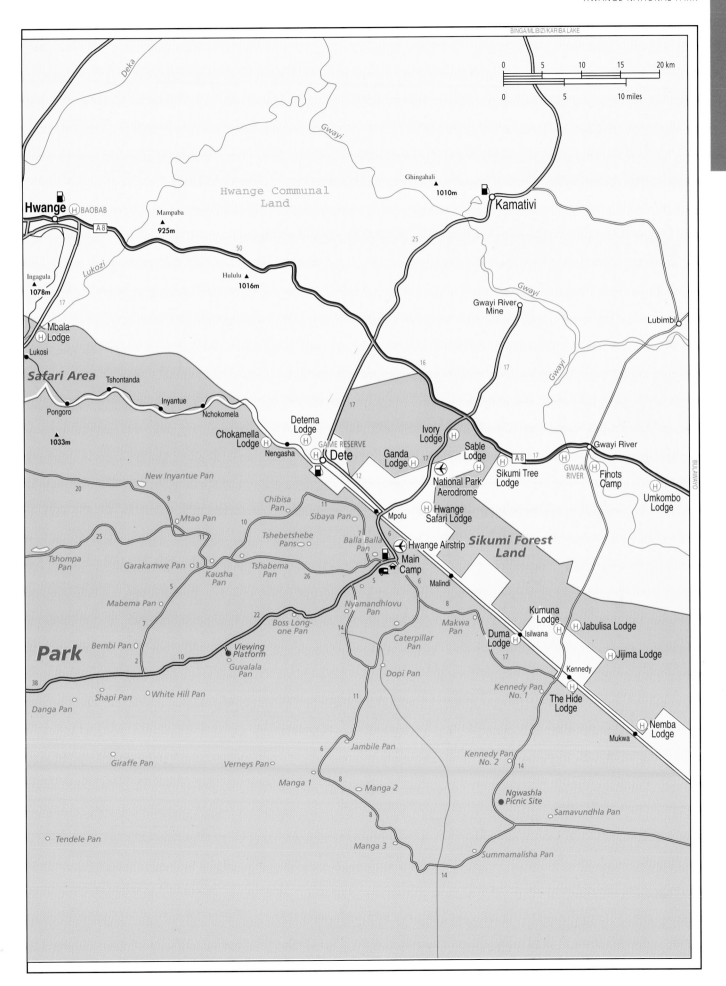

BINGA/MLIBIZI/KARIBA LAKE

Deka

Gwayi

Hwange Communal Land

Ghingahali ▲
1010m

Kamativi

Hwange ⒽBAOBAB

Mampaba ▲
925m

A 8

50

25

Lukozi

Ingagula
1078m

Hululu ▲
1016m

Gwayi

Gwayi River Mine

Lubimbi

17

16

Mbala Ⓗ Lodge

17

Lukosi

Safari Area

Tshontanda

Inyantue

Nchokomela

Gwayi

Pongoro

▲
1033m

Detema Lodge

Ivory Lodge Ⓗ

Sable Lodge Ⓗ

Gwayi River

Chokamella Ⓗ Lodge

Nengasha

GAME RESERVE
Ⓗ **Dete**

Ganda Lodge Ⓗ

17

A 8   17

GWAAI RIVER

Finots Camp Ⓗ

New Inyantue Pan

12

National Park Aerodrome ✈

Sikumi Tree Lodge Ⓗ

Umkombo Lodge Ⓗ

20

9

Chibisa Pan

11

Sibaya Pan

Mpofu

Ⓗ Hwange Safari Lodge

Mtao Pan

10

Tshebetshebe Pans

6

Sikumi Forest Land

25

11

Balla Balla Pan

Tshompa Pan

Garakamwe Pan   3

Tshabema Pan

26

✈ Hwange Airstrip

Malindi

Kausha Pan

5

5

Main Camp

8

Kumuna Lodge Ⓗ

Jabulisa Lodge Ⓗ

Mabema Pan

22

Nyamandhlovu Pan

Makwa Pan

Duma Lodge Ⓗ Isilwana

Jijima Lodge Ⓗ

Park

7

Boss Long-one Pan

14

Caterpillar Pan

8

17

Kennedy

Bembi Pan

2

10

Viewing Platform

Guvalala Pan

Dopi Pan

Kennedy Pan No. 1

Ⓗ The Hide Lodge

38

Shapi Pan

White Hill Pan

11

Nemba Lodge Ⓗ

Danga Pan

Mukwa

Giraffe Pan

6

Jambile Pan

Kennedy Pan No. 2

14

Verneys Pan

8

Manga 1

Manga 2

Ngwashla Picnic Site

Samavundhla Pan

8

Tendele Pan

Manga 3

Summamalisha Pan

14

BULAWAYO

0   5   10   15   20 km

0   5   10 miles

Matobo National Park

Much of the Matobo area to the south of Bulawayo has been set aside as a 43,000ha (106,253 acres) national park, sanctuary for white rhino and giraffe, sable, impala and an unusually large leopard population. The Matobo Hills, famed for their massive boulders and balancing rocks, are especially renowned for their birds of prey, and notably for what is believed to be the world's largest concentration of the black eagle. Graceful in flight, this magnificent raptor can often be seen hugging the precipitous cliff faces, from which it suddenly swoops down on an unwary hyrax (commonly known as a dassie or rock rabbit), its favourite prey.

The name Matobo means 'bald heads', an epithet said to have been conferred by Mzilikazi, founder of Zimbabwe's Ndebele nation, in one of his more whimsical moods: the landscape, characterized by ancient and massive granite domes, reminded him of an assembly of his aged councillors.

Among the jumble of rugged hills, too, there are *dwalas* (whale-back mountains), and caves and cliffs adorned with the paintings and engravings of those finest of prehistoric artists, the Bushmen.

It was here, in these mysterious and hauntingly beautiful hills, that the elders of the ancestral Shona communed with their great god Mwari through human oracles; here, in the 1890s, that the Ndebele warriors made their last stand against Cecil Rhodes' well-armed horsemen, and here that peace was finally negotiated at a succession of dignified *indabas*. Mzilikazi chose to be buried in the Matobos; so too did

Rhodes, whose hilltop resting place, known as World's View, is a natural amphitheatre embraced by colossal boulders.

Visitor amenities are focused on the Maleme Dam, where there are one- and two-bedroomed lodges and chalets available for hire. The road network is well maintained, and walking routes, pony trails and picnic spots have been established.

At least five of the so-called Painted Caves have been documented in detail. Especially recommended is the museum at the Pomongwe site, where thousands of Stone and Iron Age artefacts are also on display. Some of them are thought to date back as far as 14,000BC. At the Nswatugi cave there is a fine interpretive exposition of paintings, while the Inanke's decorations are exceptional in their beauty. Silozwane, just to the south of the park, contains a fascinating range of painted subjects, including a 2m (6.5ft) tall giraffe and a snake with an antelope's head.

MATOBO	J	F	M	A	M	J	J	A	S	O	N	D
AVERAGE TEMP. °F	72	70	69	66	59	54	54	59	66	70	72	70
AVERAGE TEMP. °C	22	21	21	19	15	12	12	15	19	21	22	21
Hours of Sun Daily	8	7	8	8	9	9	9	9	9	8	8	7
RAINFALL ins.	5	4	2	1	0	0	0	0	0	1.5	4	5
RAINFALL mm	134	97	50	28	7	2	1	1	8	36	99	131
Days of Rainfall	11	9	6	4	1	1	0	0	1	4	9	11

A wealth of treasures surrounds the park and includes the Bambata Caves, and Fort Usher, where Lord Baden-Powell conceived the idea of the Boy Scout Movement.

Above left: *The Matobo Hills are famed for their striking rock formations and their cliff faces.*
Top: *The last resting place of Cecil John Rhodes, sited on a Matobo hilltop known as World's View.*
Above: *One of the Matobo's myriad, brightly coloured flat lizards.*

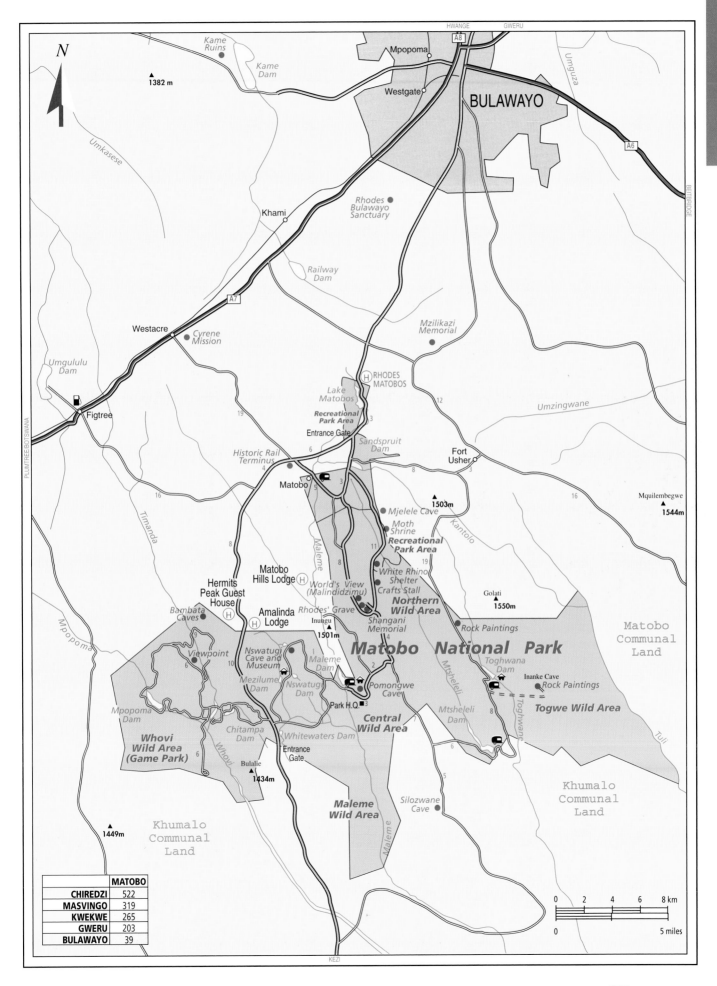

N

Kame Ruins
▲ 1382 m
Kame Dam

Mpopoma
Westgate

BULAWAYO

HWANGE   GWERU
A8

Umguza

A6

BEITBRIDGE

Umkasese

Khami
Rhodes Bulawayo Sanctuary

Railway Dam

PLUMTREE/BOTSWANA

Westacre
Cyrene Mission

Mzilikazi Memorial

A7

Umgululu Dam

Figtree

19

H RHODES MATOBOS
Lake Matobos
Recreational Park Area
Entrance Gate

Sandspruit Dam

Fort Usher

Umzingwane

12

3

Historic Rail Terminus
4

Matobo

16

Timanda

Mpopoma

8

6
5
3

8

3

Kantolo

Mjelele Cave
Moth Shrine
Recreational Park Area
White Rhino Shelter
Crafts Stall

▲ 1503m

11

19

Mquilembegwe
▲ 1544m

16

Golati
▲ 1550m

Matobo Hills Lodge   H
World's View (Malindidzimu)
Rhodes' Grave

Hermits Peak Guest House   H
Amalinda Lodge   H

Bambata Caves

Inungu
▲ 1501m

Shangani Memorial
14
2

Northern Wild Area

Rock Paintings

Matobo   National   Park

Matobo Communal Land

Viewpoint
6

8
10

Nswatugi Cave and Museum
Mezilume Dam
Nswatugi Dam
Maleme Dam

Maleme

Pomongwe Cave
Park H.Q.
3

Central Wild Area

Mtsheleli

Mtsheleli Dam

Toghwana Dam

Golati

Inanke Cave
Rock Paintings

8

Togwe Wild Area

Tuli

Mpopoma
Mpopoma Dam

Chitampa Dam
Whitewaters Dam

6

Whovi

Whovi Wild Area (Game Park)

6

Bulalie
▲ 1434m

Entrance Gate

Silozwane Cave

6

5

Khumalo Communal Land

Maleme Wild Area

Maleme

▲ 1449m

Khumalo Communal Land

	MATOBO
CHIREDZI	522
MASVINGO	319
KWEKWE	265
GWERU	203
BULAWAYO	39

0   2   4   6   8 km

0   5 miles

KEZI

17

Victoria Falls

The Victoria Falls, or 'mosi oa tunya' (smoke that thunders) as the Kololo people called it, is arguably the most spectacular of all the world's natural wonders. The volume of water that flows over the falls varies considerably, but during peak flow, between February and May, the Zambezi River thunders over the 1708m (5604ft) wide rim in a series of grand cataracts at the rate of 500,000m³ (17.6 million cu ft) per minute. The tumultuous waterfalls create a rising cloud of spray that, on a clear day, can be seen from 80km (50 miles) away. At night, during the full-moon phase, an eerie lunar rainbow arcs across the great gorge.

Visitors to the Victoria Falls can take in the awesome spectacle from a number of strategically sited viewing points, the best of which are accessible along winding paths cut through the famed 'rainforest', an enchanting place of subtropical birds, butterflies and secretive little animals, of tangled undergrowth and trees whose dense foliage glistens in the fine mist.

Above the falls is the Zambezi National Park, many of whose animals – together with a splendid array of birds – can be seen on the drive along the riverbank. Here, crocodiles bask in the sun, hippos snort and, among the high-tufted ilala palms, fish eagles cry as the sightseeing cruise vessels float gently by. These popular sundowner cruises are just one of the many ways to explore the Zambezi to either side of the falls.

Highly recommended is the trip on a small outboard-driven pontoon that glides past the lush riverine reaches, skirting the rapids and islands (largest of which is Kandahar, 10km, or 6 miles upstream) to offer superb game- and bird-viewing. More adventurous are the canoeing and rafting safaris that ply the river, both the relatively placid stretches from Kazungula eastwards to the falls, and the white waters that race through the 19 narrow gorges downstream. Other options include horseback and walking trails along the banks, and the 'Flight of Angels' light-aircraft flip over the cataracts and their surrounds.

There's plenty to see and do in the immediate vicinity of the Falls. This is Zimbabwe's prime tourist destination, served by hotels of international standard, restaurants, a modern shopping centre, curio stalls, a busy airport, and superb golfing facilities.

Special drawcards include the Crocodile Ranch and Nature Sanctuary which is home to over 2000 of the giant reptiles, and the multicultural craft village. The latter is a fascinating exposition of traditional life syles, customs, architecture, ornamentation, dance, music and drama.

There are regular performances of Makishi folk dancing – the African Spectacular – at the elegant colonial-style Victoria Falls Hotel, which first opened its doors in 1904, and visitors can also listen to the vibrant sound of *marimbas* played on the hotel's patio every lunch time. Nearby is the plush splendour of the Makasa Sun Casino Hotel.

VICTORIA FALLS	J	F	M	A	M	J	J	A	S	O	N	D
AVERAGE TEMP. °F	75	75	82	70	64	59	59	64	72	77	77	75
AVERAGE TEMP. °C	24	24	28	21	18	15	15	18	22	25	25	24
Hours of Sun Daily	7	7	8	9	10	10	10	10	10	9	7	7
RAINFALL ins.	5	5	3	1	0	0	0	0	0	3	3	5
RAINFALL mm	125	138	71	23	2	1	0	1	2	24	77	138
Days of Rainfall	14	13	7	3	1	0	0	0	1	3	10	14

Above left: *Colourful costumes, traditional music and vibrant dancing are some of the attractions of the Victoria Falls' craft village.*
Above: *The Falls, seen from the rainforest.*
Below: *Water lilies decorate the grounds of the Edwardian era Victoria Falls Hotel.*

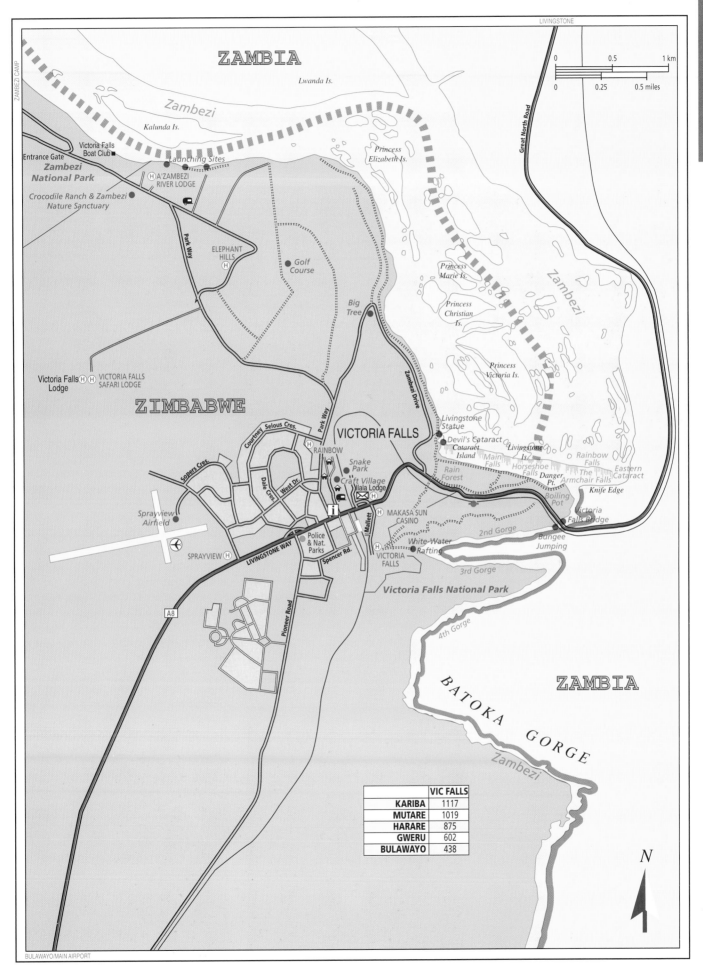

ZAMBIA

Lwanda Is.

Zambezi

Kalunda Is.

ZAMBEZI CAMP

LIVINGSTONE

Victoria Falls
Boat Club

Launching Sites

Princess
Elizabeth Is.

Entrance Gate

Zambezi
National Park

A'ZAMBEZI
RIVER LODGE

Crocodile Ranch & Zambezi
Nature Sanctuary

Great North Road

Park Way

ELEPHANT
HILLS

Golf
Course

Princess
Marie Is.

Princess
Christian
Is.

Zambezi

Big
Tree

Zambezi Drive

Victoria Falls
Lodge

VICTORIA FALLS
SAFARI LODGE

Princess
Victoria Is.

ZIMBABWE

Courtney Selous Cres.

Park Way

VICTORIA FALLS

Livingstone
Statue

RAINBOW

Sopers Cres.

Dale Cres.

West Dr.

Snake
Park

Craft Village
Ilala Lodge

Devil's Cataract
Cataract
Island

Livingstone
Is.

Main
Falls

Rain
Forest

Horseshoe
Falls

Rainbow
Falls

Eastern
Cataract

The
Armchair Falls

Knife Edge

Danger
Pt.

Sprayview
Airfield

Police
& Nat.
Parks

MAKASA SUN
CASINO

Boiling
Pot

Victoria
Falls Bridge

SPRAYVIEW

LIVINGSTONE WAY

Spencer Rd.

Mallett

VICTORIA
FALLS

White-Water
Rafting

2nd Gorge

Bungee
Jumping

A8

Pioneer Road

3rd Gorge

Victoria Falls National Park

4th Gorge

BATOKA

ZAMBIA

GORGE

Zambezi

	VIC FALLS
KARIBA	1117
MUTARE	1019
HARARE	875
GWERU	602
BULAWAYO	438

N

BULAWAYO/MAIN AIRPORT

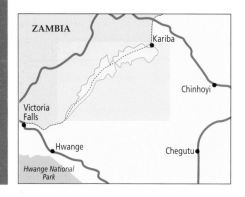

Lake Kariba

Downstream from the Victoria Falls, across one of its deepest and most precipitous gorges, the mighty Zambezi has been dammed to create an inland sea – a vast expanse of water which, until fairly recently, ranked as the world's largest man-made lake. It stretches 282km (175 miles) from end to end; to skirt its perimeter involves a 4000km (2486 miles) trip, and its usually placid, occasionally stormy, waters serve as one of Africa's most popular playgrounds. The dam, which was formally inaugurated by Queen Elizabeth the Queen Mother on 17 May 1960, is Zimbabwe's major source of electrical power.

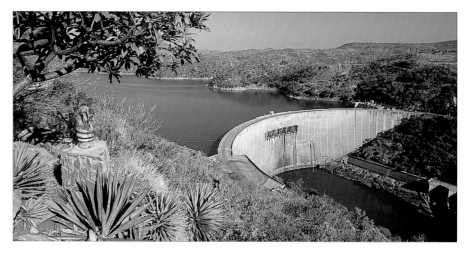

More than a million cubic metres of concrete were used in the construction of Kariba's massive dam wall during the 1950s, and over 50,000 Gwembe Tonga were displaced by the rising waters. So, too, were countless animals large and small, many of them saved from drowning by the renowned conservationist Rupert Fothergill and his rangers in an inspiring, and internationally acclaimed, exercise known as Operation Noah. The village communities and the wildlife now draw life-giving sustenance from the lake. The drowned forests of the shallows encourage a proliferation of insects and provide perches for cormorants, kingfishers, darters, herons and fish eagles.

Kariba is a magnificent wilderness of water, of lush islands and secret inlets and of charming little harbours that, together, combine to create a paradise for the yachtsman and the boating enthusiast, the fisherman and the water sportsman. And for the lover of wildlife, flanking the lake's southern shores are two of Africa's finest game sanctuaries.

The Matusadona National Park occupies nearly 1500km² (579 sq miles) of wild and scenically spectacular Zambezi escarpment countryside extending southwards from the lake's lower reaches – a pristine wilderness of bush-covered hills and woodlands that supports elephant, rhino, buffalo and a wide variety of antelope. Matusadona has two camping sites and accommodation is offered

at Ume and Mbalabala close to Tashinga, and Muuyu near Elephant Point.

Chizarira National Park, set 50km (31 miles) inland from Lake Kariba, is the finest wilderness area for backpacking in Zimbabwe. National Parks operates six exclusive camps and offers two five-day wilderness trails, and daytime walks. The park is home to sizable elephant populations, and other wildlife includes tsessebe, black rhino and zebra.

Commercial venues are dotted along and near the lake's shore and on two of its larger islands. Bumi Hills, set high on a bluff west of Matusadona National Park, and the attractively Mediterranean-style Caribbea Bay Hotel and Casino, to the east of Kariba, are the most sophisticated.

Sanyati, set in a forested river-gorge, is good for bird-watching, painting and for those who like to commune with the quieter spirits. Spurwing and Fothergill islands are for big-game aficionados, and Tiger Bay attracts the serious fisherfolk.

An enticing alternative to terrestrial living is offered by the 50 or so lake houseboats and cruisers available for charter, spacious and well appointed, even luxurious, craft that vary from six-berthers to huge multi-deck Mississippi monsters.

The Kariba Ferry is an especially attractive means of travel from one end of the lake to the other and, at the same time, of taking in some memorable sightseeing. The two largish car-ferries ply the 282km (175 miles) route between Andora harbour – a busy little place of leisure yachts and cruisers, houseboats and fishing rigs – and Mlibizi at the

western end. The voyage lasts 22 hours, and the vessels offer full bar facilities, comfortable saloon chairs (there are no cabins), good food, and superb viewing from the deck.

Fishermen come from afar to try their luck, and test their skill, on Kariba's waters. The lake is home to 22 types of bream and to carp and black bass, but the real star of the show is the tigerfish, a razor-toothed fighting species that can weigh up to 15kg (33 lb).

KARIBA	J	F	M	A	M	J	J	A	S	O	N	D
AVERAGE TEMP. °F	78	78	78	76	71	65	65	71	80	85	83	79
AVERAGE TEMP. °C	26	26	26	21	21	19	19	22	27	29	29	26
Hours of Sun Daily	7	7	7	9	10	9	10	10	10	10	8	7
RAINFALL ins.	8	6	5	1.5	0	0	0	0	0	0.5	3	7
RAINFALL mm	196	160	121	35	5	0	1	0	1	16	80	189
Days of Rainfall	17	14	10	4	1	0	0	0	0	2	8	16

Opposite top: *Kariba's dam wall, completed in the late 1950s, is 128m (420ft) high and runs 579m (1900ft) across the precipitous river-gorge that divides Zimbabwe from its northern neighbour Zambia. The hydroelectric power station is housed in a massive chamber carved out of solid rock.*

Opposite below left: *A view of Caribbea Bay marina, bright with leisure craft.*

Opposite below right: *The aristocratic fish eagle, hunter supreme. Its haunting call is the quintessential sound of Africa.*

Top: *Buffalo wallow in the shallows at the edge of the Matusadona National Park, home of Kariba's luxury safari camps, and ranked among Zimbabwe's premier game sanctuaries.*

Left: *One of Kariba's inviting tourist shops displays an array of soapstone carvings.*

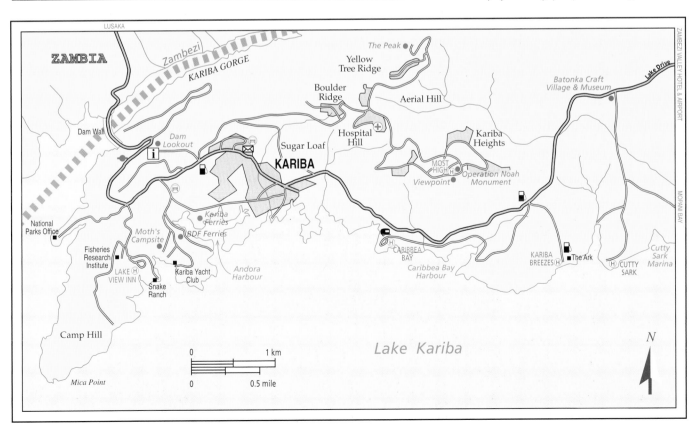

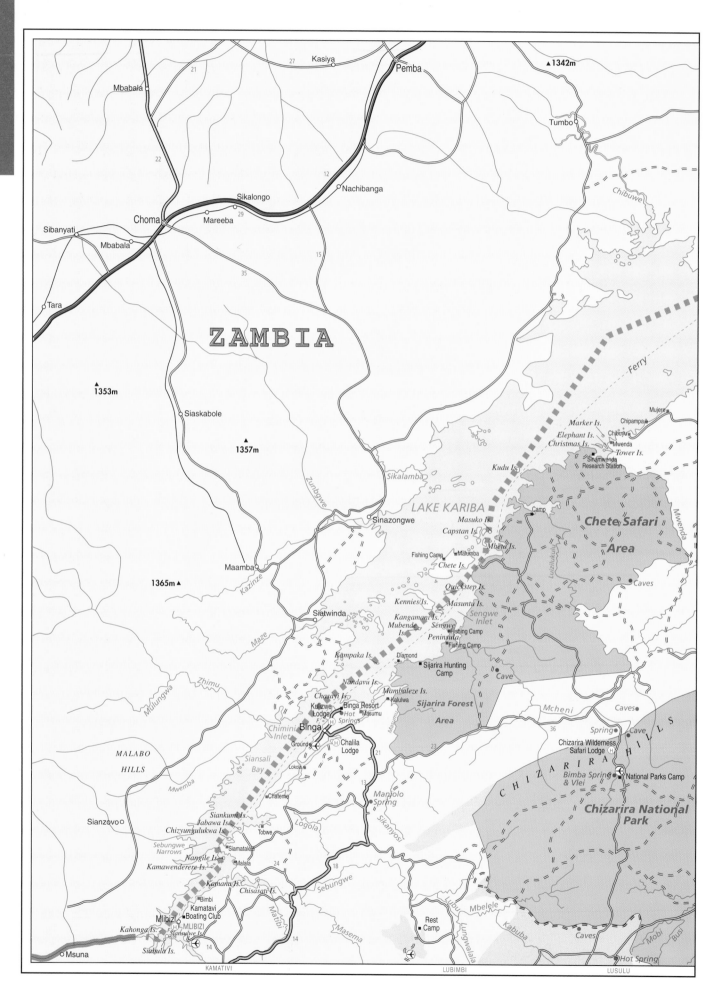

Mbabala

Kasiya

Pemba

▲1342m

Tumbo

27

21

22

12

Nachibanga

Chibuwe

Sikalongo

29

Choma

Mareeba

Ferry

Sibanyati

Mbabala

15

ZAMBIA

Tara

35

▲1353m

Siaskabole

Mujere

Marker Is.

Chipampa

Elephant Is.

Chibuyu

▲1357m

Christmas Is.

Mwenda

Tower Is.

Sinamwenda
Research Station

Kudu Is.

Sikalamba

Zumbgwye

LAKE KARIBA

Chete Safari
Area

Sinazongwe

Masuko Is.

Camp

Capstan Is.

Mbeta Is.

Fishing Camp

Malumba

Luizilukulu

Mwenda

Chete Is.

Maamba

Kazinze

Quickstep Is.

Caves

▲1365m

Kennies Is.

Masuntu Is.

Siatwinda

Kangamani Is.

Sengwe

Mubende
Is.

Sengwe
Peninsula

Inlet

Fishing Camp

Maze

Fishing Camp

Kampaka Is.

Diamond

Zhimu

Nandavu Is.

Sijarira Hunting
Camp

Cave

Mulungwa

Chasavi Is.

Mumbaleze Is.

Mcheni

Caves

Kulizwe
Lodge

Binga Resort

Kaluliwa

Sijarira Forest
Area

MALABO
HILLS

Masumu

Hot
Springs

Chimini
Inlet

Binga

Spring

Cave

Mwemba

Grounds

Chalila Lodge

36

Chizarira Wilderness
Safari Lodge

Siansali
Bay

Lokola

21

Bimba Spring
& Vlei

National Parks Camp

CHIZARIRA HILLS

Sianzovo

Chaleme

13

Manjolo
Spring

Chizarira National
Park

Siankumi Is.

Jabawa Is.

Logola

Sikanyosi

Chizyungulukwa Is.

Tobwe

Sebungwe
Narrows

Siamatalele

Nangile Is.

Malala

24

18

Kamawenderere Is.

Sebungwe

Kamana Is.

Chisasati Is.

Lubu

Mbelele

Bimbi

Kamatavi
Boating Club

Matibi

Kabuba

Mlibizi

Mobi

MLIBIZI

Masema

Rest
Camp

Caves

Kahonga Is.

Siansulwe Is.

Lungwalala

Busi

Msuna

Siabula Is.

14

14

Hot Spring

KAMATIVI

LUBIMBI

LUSULU

22

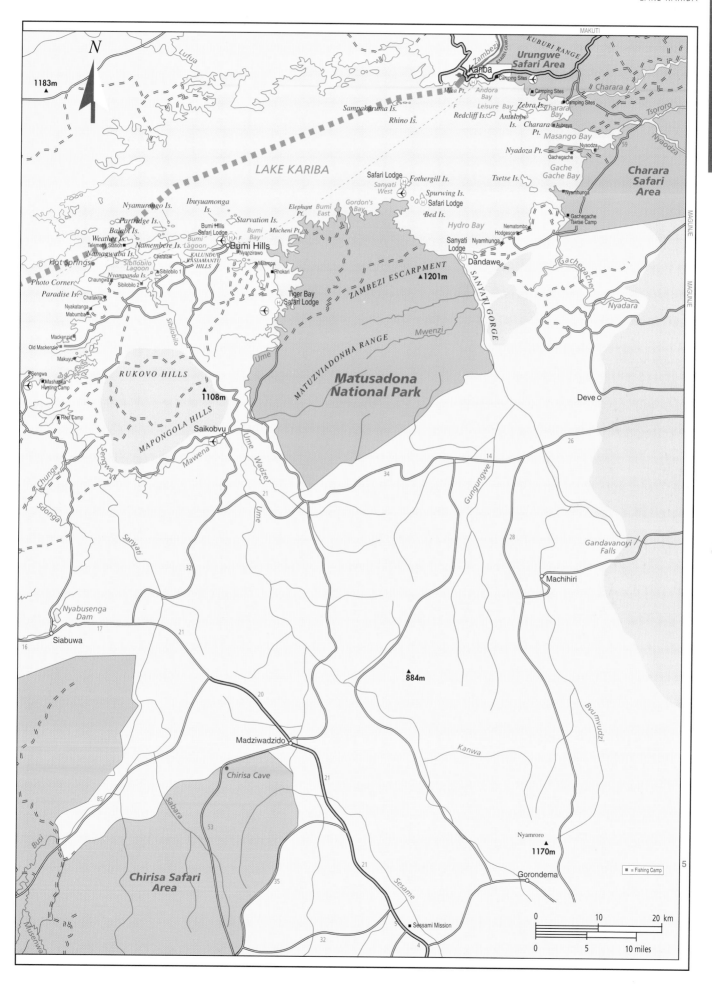

N

1183m ▲

MAKUTI

KUBURI RANGE

Urungwe
Safari Area

Kariba

Zambezi

KARIBA GORGE

Andora
Bay

Mica Pt.

Camping Sites

Charara

Camping Sites

Tsororo

Sampakaruma Is.

Rhino Is.

Redcliff Is.

Leisure Bay

Antelope
Is.

Zebra Is.

Charara
Bay

Camping Sites

Nyaodza

LAKE KARIBA

Charara
Pt.

Aubreys

Masango Bay

Nyadoza Pt.

Gachegache

Nyaodza

Gache
Gache Bay

Charara
Safari
Area

Nyamurongo Is.

Ibuyuamonga
Is.

Starvation Is.

Elephant
Pt.

Bumi
East

Gordon's
Bay

Safari Lodge

Sanyati
West

Fothergill Is.

Tsetse Is.

Spurwing Is.

Safari Lodge

Bed Is.

Nyamhunga

MAGUNJE

Purtridge Is.

Balabi Is.

Weather Is.

Namembere Is.

Namagwaba Is.

Bumi Hills
Safari Lodge

Bumi
Bay

Mucheni Pt.

Bumi
Lagoon

Hydro Bay

Nematombo

Hodgeson

Gachegache
Tsetse Camp

MAGUNJE

Bumi Hills

Sanyati
Lodge

Nyamhunga

Hot Springs

Sibilobilo
Lagoon

KALUNDU
KASIAMANTU
HILLS

Nyanzirawo

Msampa

Dandawe

Photo Corner

Paradise Is.

Chatakita

Chalala

Sibilobilo 1

Chaungwa

Nyakatanga

Maburnba

Sibilobilo

Sibilobilo 2

Nvampanda Is.

Rhokari

Tiger Bay
Safari Lodge

ZAMBEZI ESCARPMENT

▲1201m

SANYATI GORGE

Mwenzi

Nyadara

Telemetry Station

Mackenzie

Old Mackenzie

Makuyu

Ume

MATUZVIADONHA RANGE

Matusadona
National Park

Deve

Sengwa

Mashango
Hunting Camp

RUKOVO HILLS

▲1108m

Reef Camp

MAPONGOLA HILLS

Saikobvu

Mawena

Ume

Wadzi

34

26

14

Gungungwe

28

Gandavanoyi
Falls

Chunga

Sdonga

Sanyati

32

21

Ume

Machihiri

Nyabusenga
Dam

17

21

16

Siabuwa

20

884m ▲

Kanwa

Bvumvudzi

Madziwadzido

21

Chirisa Cave

Sabara

85

53

Busi

Chirisa Safari
Area

35

Sesame

Nyamroro

1170m ▲

Gorondema

■ = Fishing Camp

Musenwa

Sessami Mission

32

4

0   10   20 km

0   5   10 miles

5

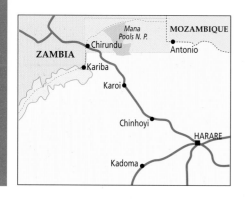

Zambezi Valley

The 300km (186 miles) stretch of the Zambezi River from below Kariba northeastwards to the Mozambique border rates as the wildest part of Zimbabwe. The great river, its islands and broad floodplains, and the woodlands, jesse bush and hills of the scenically dramatic escarpment that flanks the river's reaches, combine to form one of the last of Africa's true wilderness areas. The valley is a sanctuary for a profusion of wildlife and sustains elephant, buffalo, a myriad plains zebra and antelope, together with their attendant predators. Hippo wallow in the muddy waters and crocodile guard the river islands.

In addition, there's the small Vundu rest camp and four remote campsites, each restricted to 12 persons (two vehicles) and available on a block-booking basis.

On the park's western boundary is Ruckomechi, an exceptionally attractive 20-guest private riverside venue set among majestic mahogany and acacia trees and recently voted Zimbabwe's finest safari lodge. Elephant and buffalo wander past the thatched chalets and the bar-lounge, a companionable deck structure where guests relax at the glorious sunset hour.

Downriver, near the confluence of the Zambezi and Sapi rivers at the other end of the park, is Chikwenya Island and the Chikwenya Safari Camp, popular among true bush-lovers for its isolation, for the

Most of the Zambezi valley has been reserved for the protection of its wildlife habitats. The Mana Pools National Park covers 2200km² (850 sq miles) of a region whose most prominent features are fertile riverine terraces, formed over the centuries as the Zambezi's sluggish waters flowed northwards, leaving behind rich alluvial soils and seasonal pools around which acacia, mahogany, tamarind, fig, sausage and rain trees proliferate. In the dry season wildlife moves down from the hills, drawn by the moisture and lush vegetation.

The park has a game-viewing road network (four-wheel-drive vehicles are recommended) and, unusually, visitors are allowed to walk unaccompanied, though they must do so with extreme caution. Drifting past the Zambezi's banks in a canoe is an unforgettable way to go game-viewing. Trips can start in the narrow gorge below Kariba's dam wall and go as far as Chirundu, or as far as Mana Pools if you continue for a further three days.

The park has two pleasant public lodges, Musangu and Muchichiri, each offering furnished and equipped accommodation.

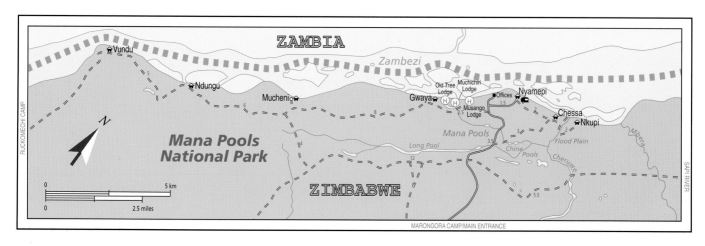

beauty of the surrounding wilderness and the deep commitment of its owners to the conservation of the environment. Visitors are housed in thatched, Batonka-style semi-open chalets – sited along the river bank to allow unrestricted views of the wide waters – and dine beneath a canopy of huge handsome trees overlooking the Zambezi and the distant plains.

Mana Pools occupies a relatively small part of the Zambezi valley; much of the rest has been set aside as proclaimed safari areas – Urungwe, Sapi, Chewore and Dande – extensive, virtually untouched wilderness expanses that are used for controlled hunting but otherwise left alone.

Opposite above: *Canoeing on the Zambezi's floodplain at Mana Pools.*
Opposite below: *Giant apple-ring thorn-trees (Acacia albida) form a dense canopy over the Chikwenya area of the valley.*
Above left: *Part of the valley's pleasant Musangu Lodge.*
Above: *Reaching for the tastiest top shoots.*
Left: *Zebra are prominent among the teeming wildlife that during the rainy season moves down from the hills that flank the Zambezi River.*

ZAMBEZI VALLEY	J	F	M	A	M	J	J	A	S	O	N	D
AVERAGE TEMP. °F	78	78	78	76	71	65	65	71	80	85	83	79
AVERAGE TEMP. °C	26	26	26	21	21	19	19	22	27	29	29	26
Hours of Sun Daily	7	7	7	9	10	9	10	10	10	10	8	7
RAINFALL ins.	8	6	5	1.5	0	0	0	0	0	0.5	3	7
RAINFALL mm	196	160	121	35	5	0	1	0	1	16	80	189
Days of Rainfall	17	14	10	4	1	0	0	0	0	2	8	16

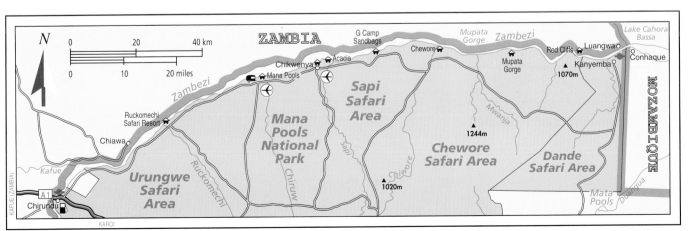

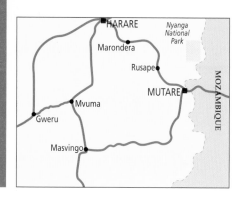

Nyanga National Park

For sheer scenic beauty there are few regions of Africa that can compete with the high mountain rampart that runs down Zimbabwe's eastern border. It stretches for 300km (186 miles) in three mountain groups – Nyanga, Bvumba and Chimanimani – to divide the highveld of Zimbabwe from Mozambique's tropical lowland plain. Nyanga is the northernmost part, much of it protected within a national park – an enchanting expanse of rugged hills, pine forests, waterfalls, rivers and swathes of moorland slopes. Its lakes – Rhodes, Udu and Nyangwe – are fringed by reedbeds and lilies, and overlooked by sweeps of mountain terrain.

The park attracts walkers, pony-trekkers and climbers. Highest of the peaks and a favourite ascent (a two-hour hike to the top has been charted) is Mount Nyangani, which soars 2593m (8508ft) above sea level and dominates the skyline, its crest often mantled in cloud, its distinctive form discernible from a distance of 100km (62 miles).

Tucked against the mountain's flank is the Nyazengu Nature Reserve, known for its proteas and other wild flowers, its salmon-trout pools, its wildlife – lion and leopard have been spotted – and for its walking trail. This last meanders through montane forest, and then grassland and more forest, to emerge onto a plateau, thereafter descending through a fairyland of trees and streams.

On the Nyanga plateau one can see the debris of ancient iron workings. Other, more prominent relics of long-gone days are scattered throughout the park – stone-walled hilltop enclosures that once served as corrals, stock-pits and 'kopje forts', and terraces designed to retain the precious soil in this mountainous region of heavy rains.

Special points of interest are the ruins at Nyahokwe and the Ziwa field museum, surrounded by the stone structures of a community of iron-smelting craftsmen, builders and farmers that lived here about 300 years ago. There are picnic shelters nearby.

Of the park's 17 rivers, the Pungwe is the largest. Its 10km (6 mile) gorge is lushly vegetated, and its waterfall, tumbling over the escarpment's lip in an explosive tumult of water, is most spectacular.

The cataract is rivalled, however, by the Mutarazi Falls, set in the Mutarazi National Park at the southern end of the Nyanga mountains. The falls plunge, in two stages, 760m (2494ft) to the lovely, fertile Honde valley below. The vistas from the lofty promontory are breathtaking. A National Parks campsite offering basic facilities is situated above the falls.

The Nyanga region is well developed for tourism. The roads are generally in excellent condition and accommodation is plentiful. Especially attractive is Troutbeck Inn, an enchanting resort hotel that is situated beneath National Trust's World's View and the Connemara lakes. It has a trout-stocked dam, golf course, charmingly appointed rooms, and a foyer log fire.

Nyanga is fine trout-fishing country; the upland dams and clear, ice-cold streams are stocked from the local hatchery, the country's largest. The average catch is around 1kg

(just over 2 lb); the record is 3.8kg (8.4 lb). The best rivers are the Nyamaziwa and the Nyangombe, and the Gulliver and Purdon are good quality dams.

Below left: *Fishing for trout in the cold, clear waters of a Nyanga dam.*
Bottom: *The magnificent vista westwards, across the highveld plain, from Nyanga's World's View.*
Below: *Nyanga's famed Troutbeck Inn, which boasts its own lake and golf course.*

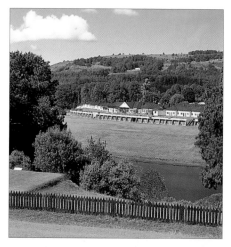

NYANGA	J	F	M	A	M	J	J	A	S	O	N	D
AVERAGE TEMP. °F	63	63	61	59	55	52	52	54	59	63	63	63
AVERAGE TEMP. °C	17	17	16	15	13	11	11	12	15	17	17	17
Hours of Sun Daily	6	6	7	8	8	8	8	9	9	9	7	6
RAINFALL ins.	10	10	6	2	1	1	0.5	1	2	5	10
RAINFALL mm	255	255	165	60	20	18	14	20	51	128	245
Days of Rainfall	19	18	16	9	5	5	5	4	2	7	12	19

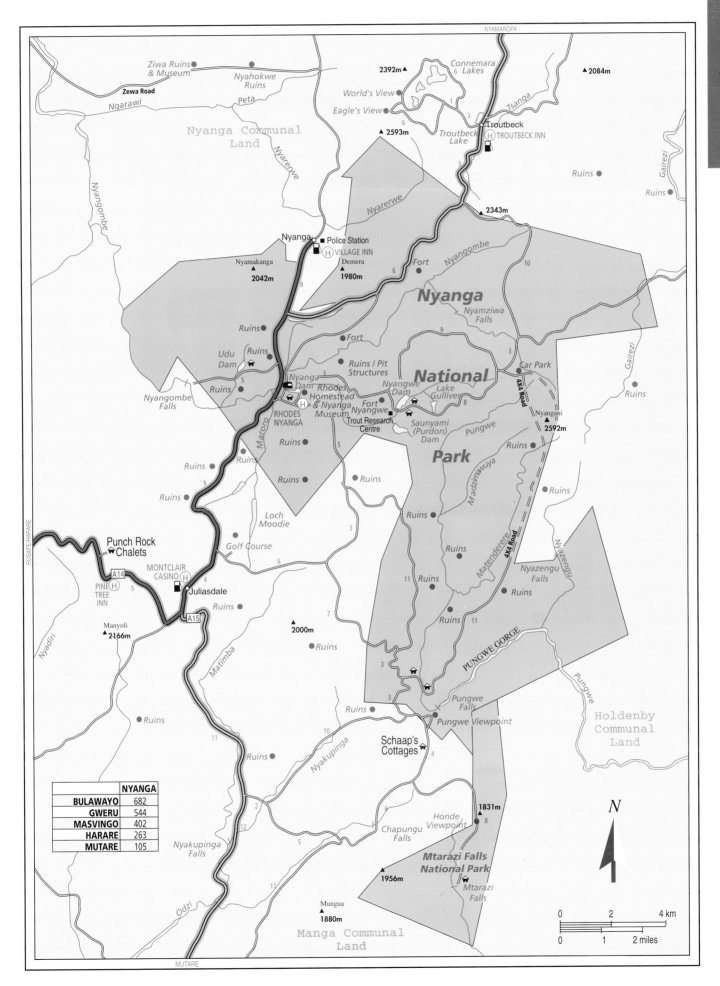

	NYANGA
BULAWAYO	682
GWERU	544
MASVINGO	402
HARARE	263
MUTARE	105

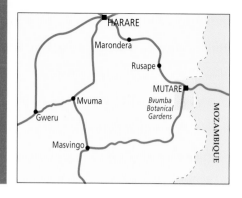

Mutare Area

No town in Zimbabwe can match Mutare for visual attractiveness and the enchantment of its setting. Located in a natural amphitheatre of the Sakubva river-valley, it is girded on all sides by the splendour of forested hills, and for much of the year its streets and suburbs are ablaze with the glory of jacaranda and flame trees and multicoloured bougainvillea. Mutare serves both as the exit point for travellers to the northern Mozambican port of Beira, across the lowland plain to the east, and as the gateway to Zimbabwe's eastern highlands – Nyanga to the north (see page 26), the Bvumba and Chimanimani mountains (see page 30) to the south.

MUTARE	J	F	M	A	M	J	J	A	S	O	N	D
AVERAGE TEMP. °F	73	70	68	68	63	57	57	61	63	66	70	73
AVERAGE TEMP. °C	23	21	20	20	17	14	14	16	17	19	21	23
Hours of Sun Daily	6	6	7	8	8	8	8	9	9	9	7	6
RAINFALL ins.	65	61	33	11	5	3	2	3	8	16	36	65
RAINFALL mm	165	157	86	28	13	8	5	7	20	41	92	165
Days of Rainfall	13	13	9	8	2	2	2	2	2	5	9	12

Travellers approaching Mutare from the east cut through Christmas Pass, from which there are fine views of the little city. An even more breathtaking panorama unfolds as you make your way up the gravel road leading to the 1520m (4987ft) crest of Mutare Heights.

Until fairly recently Christmas Pass was graced by a monument to Kingsley Fairbridge, a South African-born Rhodes scholar and poet who launched, at the turn-of-the-century, a scheme to settle disadvantaged British children in various parts of the Empire (including Zimbabwe, which was then known as Rhodesia). The monument, unveiled by Queen Elizabeth (today the Queen Mother) in 1953, was removed after independence in 1980 and now resides in Mutare's Utopia Museum, located in the house where Fairbridge was born, and whose various exhibits depict the lifestyles of the region's early white settlers.

Among the area's prime attractions is La Rochelle, an elegant private residence, 13km (8 miles) from town, bequeathed to the nation by wealthy philanthropists Sir Stephen and Lady Courtauld. La Rochelle's 14ha (35 acre) tiered gardens are graced by an exquisite show of orchids, rare trees and ornamental shrubs.

To the south are the Bvumba mountains, a mist-wreathed and beautifully forested range traversed by a road that starts at Mutare's industrial sites and ends among the coffee plantations beyond the handsome, pink-turreted Leopard Rock Hotel, which is framed and shaded by ancient gnarled trees. The entrance foyer of black marble and white Grecian columns has a two-storey-high glass panel offering a splendid view of a botanical wonderland, and the hotel's rooms are Camelot-sumptuous.

The Bvumba region offers some splendid scenic drives. Recommended destinations include the fertile Burma valley and the Bvumba Botanical Gardens.

The latter encompass a 30ha (74 acres) English-country garden of azaleas, fuchsias, hydrangeas and annuals in superbly land-scaped grounds embellished with pathways, pools, streams and wooden bridges. The Bunga Botanical Reserve, close by, is notable for its indigenous rainforest.

Above left: *The little garden city of Mutare, superbly set among the Mtanda mountains.*
Above: *A charming example of colonial architecture in Mutare's Herbert Chitepo Street.*
Left: *The sculptured elegance of the Bvumba Botanical Gardens, to the south of Mutare.*

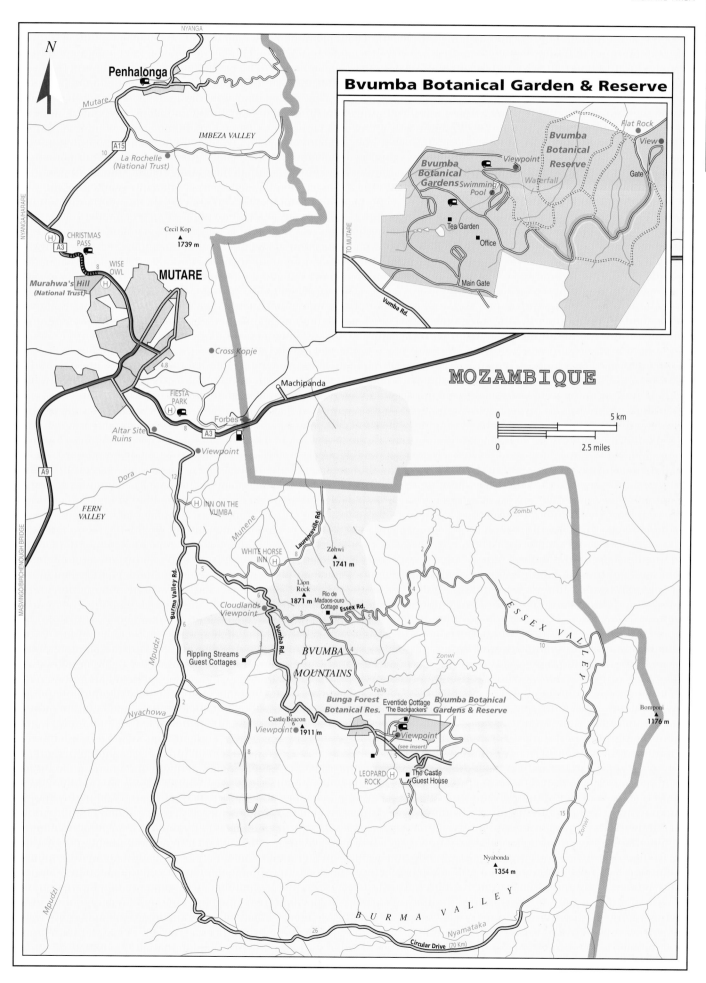

N

Penhalonga

Mutare

NYANGA

IMBEZA VALLEY

A15

10

La Rochelle
(National Trust)

Cecil Kop
▲
1739 m

CHRISTMAS
PASS
A3

WISE
OWL

8

Murahwa's Hill
(National Trust)

MUTARE

● Cross Kopje

4.8

FIESTA
PARK

Machipanda

Altar Site
Ruins ●

Forbes

8

A3

A9

● *Viewpoint*

Dora

12

FERN
VALLEY

INN ON THE
VUMBA

Munene

WHITE HORSE
INN

8

Zohwi
▲
1741 m

5

Lion
Rock
▲
1871 m

Rio de
Madaos-ouro
Cottage

Essex Rd.

Cloudlands
Viewpoint

3

5

Rippling Streams
Guest Cottages ■

BVUMBA

4

Zonwi

MOUNTAINS

Falls

Nyachowa

2

Bunga Forest
Botanical Res.

Eventide Cottage
'The Backpackers'

Bvumba Botanical
Gardens & Reserve

Castle Beacon
▲
1911 m

Viewpoint ●

Viewpoint
(see insert)

8

LEOPARD
ROCK

The Castle
Guest House

3

MASVINGO/BIRCHENOUGH BRIDGE

NYANGA—HARARE

Burma Valley Rd.

Vumba Rd.

Mpudzi

Mpudzi

MOZAMBIQUE

Zombi

2

ESSEX VALLEY

4

10

Bomponi
▲
1176 m

15

Zonwi

Nyabonda
▲
1354 m

BURMA VALLEY

Nyamataka

Circular Drive (70 Km)

26

0 ——————— 5 km
0 ——————— 2.5 miles

Bvumba Botanical Garden & Reserve

Bvumba
Botanical
Reserve

Flat Rock ●

● View

Viewpoint ●

Bvumba
Botanical
Gardens

Waterfall

Gate

Swimming
Pool ●

Tea Garden

■ Office

TO MUTARE

Main Gate

Vumba Rd.

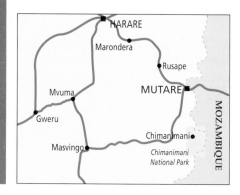

Chimanimani

Almost the entire length of eastern Zimbabwe's southernmost mountain range is encompassed within the Chimanimani National Park, a magical region of craggy massifs, deep valleys, streams and waterfalls, of forest, grassland and heath. The region's highest peaks – Kweza, Mawenje and Dombe – rise more than 2200m (7218ft) above the surrounding countryside. The park is known more for its scenic beauty than for its wildlife. Even so, it has its animals, the largest of which is the eland. Baboons are common, shy blue duiker can sometimes be spotted, and agile klipspringers scale the rocky outcrops.

Above: *The Chimanimani National Park is a lovely region of rugged terrain and deep, wooded valleys of undisturbed fauna and flora.*
Below: *The delicate tracery of the Bridal Veil Falls, within the Chimanimani's eland sanctuary.*

Like Nyanga and the Bvumba mountains to the north, this is fine walking terrain. Indeed, most of the park is accessible only by foot, and it is crisscrossed by pathways, some of the more interesting ones leading to Skeleton Pass, the Southern Lakes (this is known as the Banana Grove trail), and to the wildness of the Bundi plateau.

There is the three-hour climb up to Mount Binga (2437m; 7996ft), and the rock formations and enchanted waters of Tessa's Pool will refresh you en route to the Mutekeswane Base Camp, the usual entry point into the mountains. Chimanimani also boasts some of the earth's deepest caves; one of them – the Jungle Pot – tunnels 250m (820ft) down into the ground.

At the southern extremity of the park, in a valley that nudges the Mozambique border, are the two Haroni Rusitu botanical reserves, splendid showcases of rainforest, small mammals such as the tree civet, and a rich birdlife that includes the chestnut-fronted helmet shrike and red-winged warbler.

To the west of the park and close to the tiny village of Chimanimani is the eland sanctuary, an expanse of mountainous terrain that serves as haven to a remnant population of the species (which is the only large antelope to thrive among pine plantations), together with a number of waterbuck and zebra. It also embraces the exquisite Bridal Veil Falls.

South of the small lowveld farming centre of Chipinge (*see* page 57) you'll find the Chirinda Forest Botanical Reserve, centrepiece of which is the mission station of Mount Selinda. Chirinda contains one of the country's last patches of primeval forest and some magnificent hardwood trees – more than 100 species in all, including ironwoods and red mahoganies. One specimen, a 1000-year-old red mahogany, is nearly 60m (197ft) high and 16m (52ft) in circumference.

CHIMANIMANI	J	F	M	A	M	J	J	A	S	O	N	D
AVERAGE TEMP. °F	66	63	63	61	57	54	52	55	61	64	64	64
AVERAGE TEMP. °C	19	17	17	16	14	12	11	13	16	18	18	18
Hours of Sun Daily	7	6	6	7	7	7	7	8	9	8	7	7
RAINFALL ins.	97	118	83	36	18	17	14	13	11	23	50	102
RAINFALL mm	245	299	211	92	45	44	36	33	28	59	127	261
Days of Rainfall	16	16	15	9	7	6	6	5	5	5	12	17

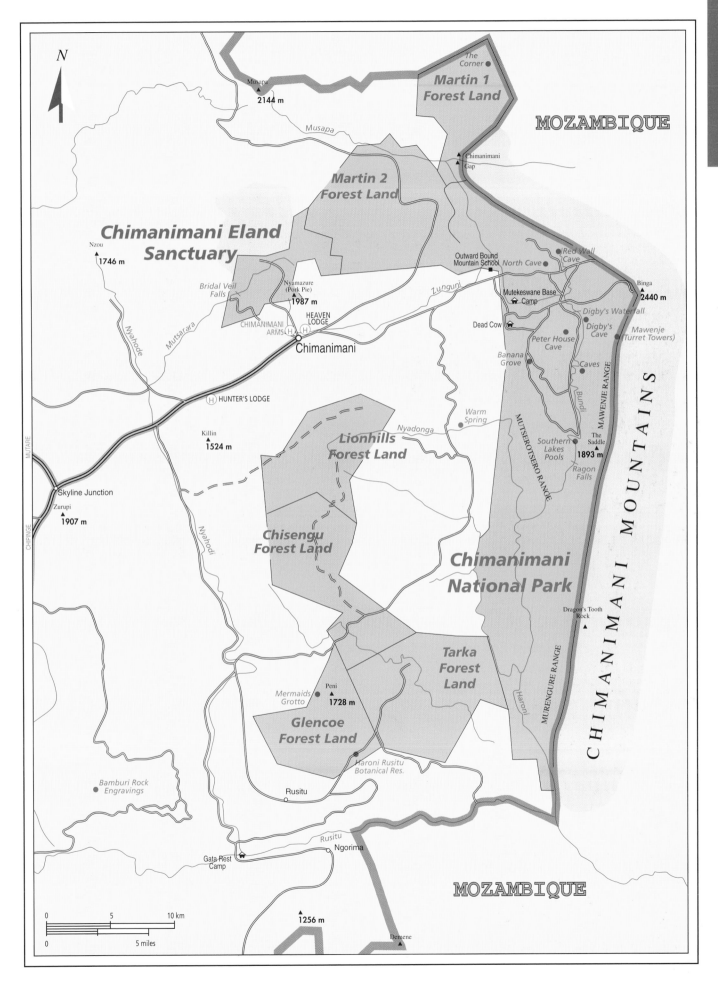

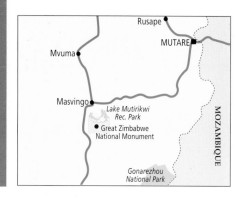

Great Zimbabwe

After the Victoria Falls, the ruins of Great Zimbabwe are, for many visitors, the country's greatest single attraction. The high-walled granite structures that rise from the Mutirikwi river-valley, to the southeast of Masvingo, functioned as the heart of the great 13th-century Karangan empire and the centrepiece of a settlement thought to number some 40,000 people. These were the Shona-speaking ancestors of modern Zimbabweans. They were farmers and traders, drawing their wealth mainly from cattle, and from the deposits of gold that lay close to the surface of the ground, and they ranked as the finest of sub-Saharan Africa's early architects.

The Karangan kings ruled over a vast region between the Limpopo and Zambezi rivers until the beginning of the 17th century, their power and wealth derived from gold and iron, massive herds of cattle and the crops of a fertile land, and from commercial relations that extended far beyond the shores of southern Africa. Great Zimbabwe was the largest and most flourishing of the citadels.

Pride of place among the ancient ruins is taken by the Great Enclosure, whose million or so interlocking blocks of granite (mortar was unknown in those days, which makes its construction an even more remarkable feat of engineering) combine to create a circular wall 11m (36ft) high and 243m (797ft) in circumference. The enclosure accommodated the homes of the royal household which, built of *daga* (clay earth), pole and thatch, have long since disappeared.

Much more solid is the enclosure's conical tower, reminiscent of a giant grain basket and symbol of abundance. A narrow passage gives access to the tower area.

Across the park-like valley, set at the edge of a cliff, is the Hill Complex, oldest of the ruins and the area in which the more important of the Karangan notables lived. Nearby are other excavated sites, including a metal smelting area, and a place of obvious ritual significance from which eight carved soapstone birds (stylized representations, it's thought, of the fish eagle) were unearthed. The 'Zimbabwe bird' is now one of the country's national symbols.

The ordinary people of the settlement were spread out on the periphery of the Hill Complex and in the valley below, where one can still see, among the profusion of ruins, the remains of their domestic enclosures.

Close to the ruins is a reconstructed Karangan village and the Great Zimbabwe Museum, whose intriguing displays include a miniature walk-through replica of the ruins, and exhibits relating to the earlier San (Bushman) hunter-gatherers, the original inhabitants of the area; to the Iron Age people who followed them 1700 years ago, and of course to the Karangan culture as well.

Among specific exhibits are some of the famous soapstone birds, tools, royal regalia, and a collection of Oriental trade goods.

GREAT ZIMBABWE	J	F	M	A	M	J	J	A	S	O	N	D
AVERAGE TEMP. °F	73	72	70	68	61	57	55	61	66	72	73	73
AVERAGE TEMP. °C	23	22	21	20	16	14	13	16	19	22	23	23
Hours of Sun Daily	7	7	7	8	9	8	8	9	9	8	7	7
RAINFALL ins.	5	4.5	2	1	1	0	0	0	0.5	1	3	6
RAINFALL mm	146	117	68	25	12	6	2	3	10	26	89	154
Days of Rainfall	12	12	8	5	3	3	1	2	2	5	9	13

Opposite above: *One of the famed carved soapstone 'Zimbabwe birds'.*

Right: *The distinctive conical tower (believed to represent a grain basket, symbol of abundance) inside the Great Enclosure. The three main components of the ruined city – Hill Complex, valley complex and Great Enclosure – were built between AD1000 and 1200.*

Opposite below: *The view from the Hill Complex to the Great Enclosure.*

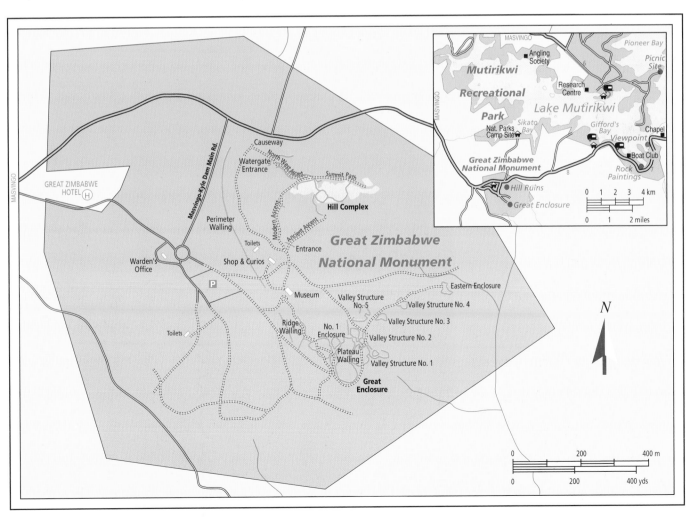

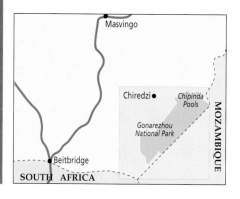

Gonarezhou National Park

Some 5000km² (1930 sq miles) of dry, sun-scorched lowveld plain in the southeast of the country has been set aside as the Gonarezhou National Park, a name that means 'place of elephants'. And indeed the elephants are there, in abundance – more than 6000 of them roam this ruggedly remote mopane and baobab region. Their very presence in such numbers is remarkable, because the wildlife of the wider area has suffered grievously from relentless drought, from massive poaching and from a protracted civil war fought just across the border in neighbouring Mozambique.

Gonarezhou is, potentially, one of Africa's finest conservation areas. It still has its problems – the elephants themselves cause a great deal of environmental damage, which is compounded by bush-burning and the diversion of the river waters for irrigation – but remains nevertheless a magnificent wilderness destination.

Though not prolific, the other wildlife populations are varied, encompassing among much else buffalo, giraffe, zebra, hippo, crocodile, the rare Lichtenstein's hartebeest, the shy suni, the nyala and many more types of antelope. The carnivores include lion and leopard.

Gonarezhou's major river, and Zimbabwe's largest internal watercourse, is the Save. Also prominent is the Runde, which rises near the Midlands city of Gweru to flow down through the lowveld irrigation complex and then meanders past the dramatic red sandstone Chilojo Cliffs to join the Save in a swampy area at the park's eastern end – a water wonderland for bird-watchers.

On the Save, to the north, is the Chivirira Falls and east of the Runde is Machiniwa Pan with its winterthorn and dense riverine forest. It is the Runde River that provides the scenic backcloth for many of Gonarezhou's best wildlife viewing areas. There are well developed campsites at Chipinda Pools and Chinguli, and others including the Chilojo Cliffs are dotted along the river's banks.

Picnic sites have been established, and the fishing is excellent. Boating, however, is not permitted even though at certain times of the year specific parts of the Runde are navigable. Note, too, that this is an endemic malaria area, so take the necessary precautions.

Chipinda Pools is the headquarters of the park's northern section, which has its own road network (a four-wheel-drive is not essential, but recommended). So too does the Mabalauta section to the south, focus of which is the pleasant Swimuwini rest camp which overlooks the Mwenezi River's buffalo bend. Here the wildlife is much in evidence; large game and the occasional lion can sometimes be seen around the grounds. The Mabalauta area has five campsites.

Wildlife is also attracted to many of the pans that radiate from the Mwenezi River. These include Ironwood, together with Manyanda which has a viewing platform, Mafuku and Manjinji.

Opposite top: *The broad reaches of the Save River, which joins the Runde along Gonarezhou's eastern flank. Extensive wetlands at the confluence are rich in birdlife during the rainy season.*

Opposite below left: *A giant baobab – known as the 'upside down tree' and prominent in African folklore – rises from the grassland plain on the Lone Star Ranch, adjacent to Gonarezhou.*

Opposite below right: *The dramatically sculpted red sandstone Chilojo Cliffs line a long stretch of the Runde River.*

Right: *A kudu and her calf race for cover.*

GONAREZHOU	J	F	M	A	M	J	J	A	S	O	N	D
AVERAGE TEMP. °F	72	70	69	66	59	54	54	59	66	70	72	70
AVERAGE TEMP. °C	22	21	21	19	15	12	12	15	19	21	22	21
Hours of Sun Daily	8	7	8	8	9	9	9	9	8	8	8	7
RAINFALL ins.	5	4	2	1	0	0	0	0	1.5	4	5	
RAINFALL mm	134	97	50	28	7	2	1	8	36	99	131	
Days of Rainfall	11	9	6	4	1	1	0	0	1	4	9	11

Main Map Section Key and Legend

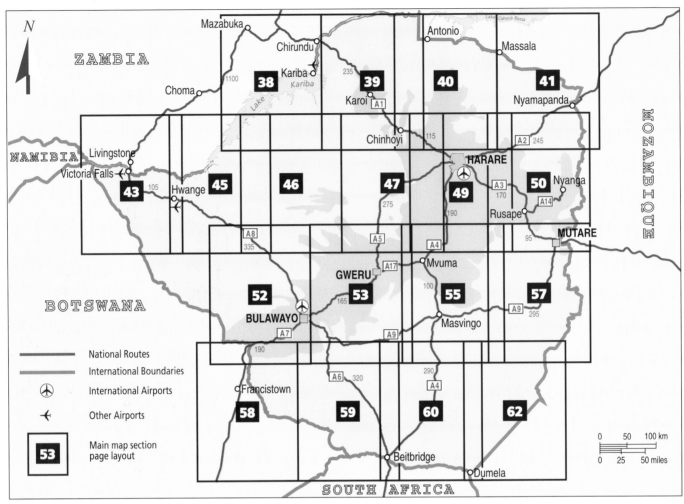

	National Routes
	International Boundaries
✈	International Airports
✈	Other Airports
53	Main map section page layout

Main Map section
Scale 1: 950,000

Border posts			Buildings of interest	
National roads			Grenzübergang	
Nationalrouten		Poste de contrôle		

National roads
Nationalrouten
Route nationale

Principal roads
Nationalstraßen
Route de liaison régionale

Main roads
Hauptstraßen
Route principale
Tar   Untar

Minor roads
Nebenstraßen
Route secondaire
Tar   Untar

Tracks
Sandweg
Piste

Footpath
Wanderwege
Circuit de randonnée

Route numbers
Routenummern
Numéro de route
A4

Distances
Entfernungen
Distance
19 // 15

Railways
Eisenbahn
Chemin de fer

International boundary
Landesgrenzen
Frontière internationale

Border posts
Grenzübergang
Poste de contrôle
Chirundu

Scenic routes
Malerische Landschaft
Route panoramique

Mountain passes
Bergpässe
Col
Moodies

Game & nature reserves
Wild und Naturschutzgebiete
Réserve naturelle
Hwange N.P.

Mountain ranges
Gebirge
Chaîne de montagnes
WEDZA

Airports
Flughäfen
Aéroport
✈ INT.   ✈ Other

Cities
Großstadt
Grande ville
☐

Towns
Stadt
Ville secondaire
◉

Small towns
Kleinstadt
Petite ville
○

Villages
Dorf
Petit village
○

Buildings of interest
Wichtige Bauwerke
Monument à voir
■

Major petrol stops
Große Tankstelle
Station-service

Hotels (selected)
Hotel (Auswahl)
Hôtel
Ⓗ

Camps
Ferienlager
Camp

Caravan parks
Wohwagenpark
Camping-caravaning

Places of interest
Sehenswürdigkeiten
Endroit à voir
Ruins ●

Stations (selected)
Bahnhof (Auswahl)
Gare
●

Area names
Gebiet
Nom de la région
Matobo

Peaks in metres
Höhe in Metern
Sommet
Dombo
2005m
▲

Water features
Gewässer
Hydrographie

Eastern Kariba and Zambezi Valley

The Zambezi River Valley is dominated by the 5000km² (1930 sq miles) Lake Kariba, a prime recreational area and a valuable source of protein for the local inhabitants: around 8000 tonnes of a small sardine-like fish known as kapenta are harvested from the waters each year. The waters are also home to many other species, notably bream and the feisty tigerfish, much prized by the sporting anglers who are drawn to the area. The concrete-arch dam wall, which straddles the gorge to connect Zimbabwe with Zambia, incorporates a hydroelectric power plant that supplies the two countries with about 7000 million kilowatt hours of electricity each year.

The main tourist attractions of this splendid region (*see* pages 38 and 39) include boating, canoeing, fishing, watersports, game-viewing and bird-watching. The area is well served by resorts, hotels, private safari lodges and camping grounds. Access is via the tarred A1 highway that leads northwest from Harare to Makuti, where you branch westwards for Kariba town.

Kariba town Kariba, set among the hills overlooking the dam wall, was built in the 1950s to house engineering and construction workers (many of them Italian) employed on the wall and power station.

It has a modern shopping complex, supermarket, bakery, and some smart houses and a hotel in the 'Heights' area.

Well worth a visit are the nearby crocodile farm, and the attractively unusual Church of St Barbara. Erected in honour of those who died building the dam, it has an 'open' circular shape, featuring a series of archways in place of walls.

Fothergill and Spurwing islands
Set close to the Matusadona National Park's lake shore, these two islands are large enough to sustain their own game populations. Each has a safari camp of comfortably appointed thatched chalets, cabins and huts (Spurwing's accommodation is in the ethnic Batonka style), a dining area and bar.

Professional guides conduct guests on game drives through Matusadona's grasslands and mopane woods, and on fishing trips, bush walks and lake excursions either by power boat, canoe or pontoon.

Matusadona National Park
A magnificent lakeside and escarpment wilderness (*see* page 20) whose undulating, bush-covered hills are home to splendid populations of elephant, buffalo, zebra, eland, kudu, waterbuck, impala, together with lion, leopard and spotted hyena.

The human presence tends to be concentrated along the shoreline, an aquatic delight of bays, inlets, river estuaries and offshore islands much favoured by fishermen and bird-watchers. Visitors can stay at one or other of the three small rest-camps and two camping sites, or at nearby Bumi Hills.

Bumi Hills Lodge A luxurious safari venue (technically a three-star hotel) sited high on a ridge at the western end of the Matusadona park (*see* page 20).

Guests are treated to superb views of the lake, especially at sunrise and sunset. The lodge offers well-appointed en suite rooms, an excellent à la carte restaurant, game drives and sundowner cruises.

Safari areas Vast, unspoilt expanses of this region are given over to the preservation of the game-rich wilderness of northern Zimbabwe. Visitor facilities are limited, and hunting takes place on a strictly controlled basis. The 1700km² (656 sq miles) Charara Safari Area on Lake Kariba's eastern shore offers excellent game-viewing (but beware of elephant and lion along the roads), fishing and a rest-camp.

The middle Zambezi areas are the Urungwe, the Sapi, the Chewore, the Dande and, to the south, the Doma. These and the Mana Pools National Park have collectively been declared a World Heritage Site (*see* page 25).

Mana Pools National Park
The principal features of this outstanding wilderness (*see* page 24) are the wide, lush

Above: *The view from Bumi Hills, one of Kariba's more luxurious safari venues.*
Below left: *The attractive lakeside camp on Kariba's Spurwing Island. Accommodation comprises rustic chalets and cabins, and tents under thatch. The camp's social hub is its central complex of dining area and a two-storey, gazebo-type pub.*

riverine terraces and their pools; the huge number and variety of large game, including elephant, buffalo, plains zebra, a myriad antelope, and the prolific avifauna, notably waterbirds and a splendid array of raptors. The best time to visit the park is during the dry season, and especially in October when the wildlife is concentrated near water. Boating is permitted, and game-viewing canoe safaris are on offer.

Accommodation is available at the two public eight-bed rest-camps, Musangu and Muchichiri, and at private safari venues, including Ruckomechi, Chikwenya and the tented Camp Zambezi.

Chirundu The little border town of Chirundu marks the exit point for motorists travelling north and is situated on the quickest land-link between Harare and Lusaka, 125km (78 miles) beyond the border. The swift-flowing Zambezi is crossed via the 415m (1362ft) Otto Beit Bridge. Visitor facilities are limited.

37

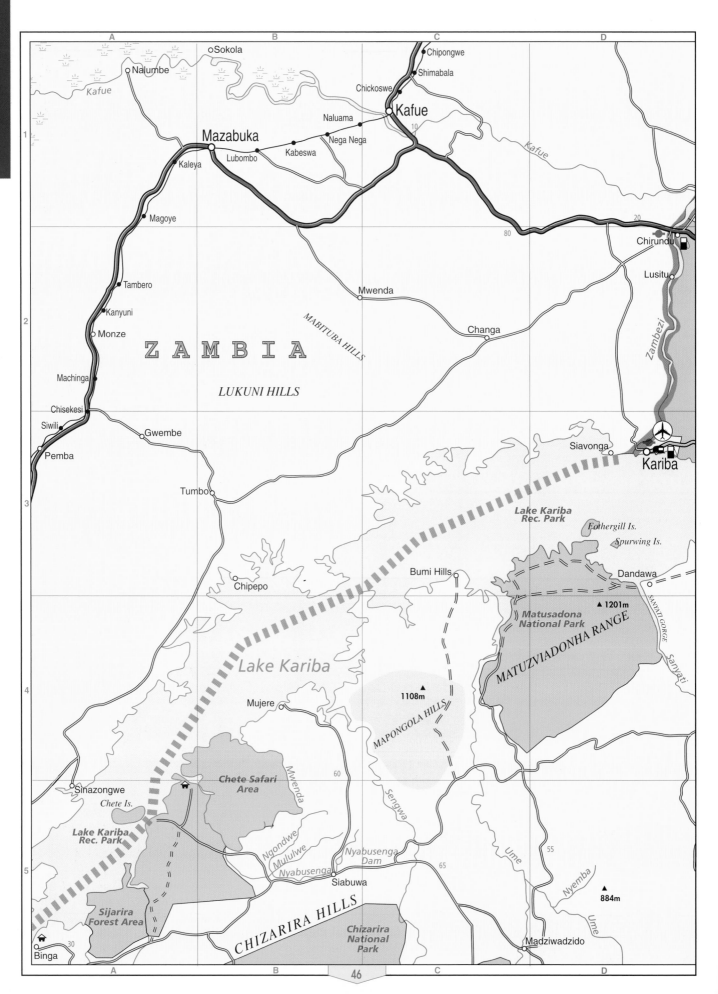

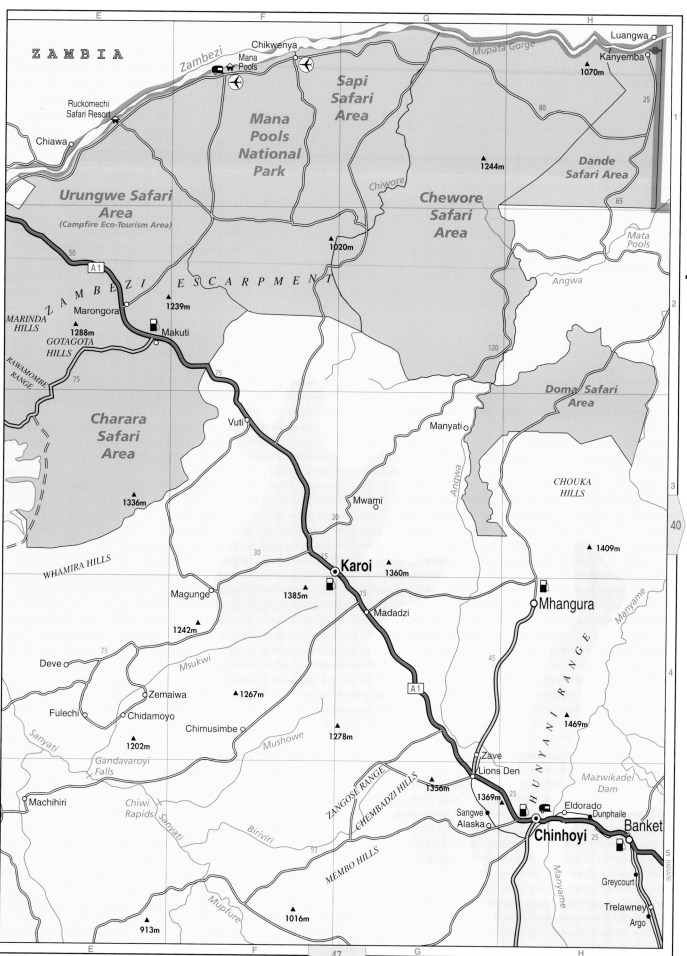

Z A M B I A

Zambezi

Chikwenya

Mana Pools

Sapi Safari Area

Mupata Gorge

Luangwa

Kanyemba

▲ 1070m

Dande Safari Area

Ruckomechi Safari Resort

Chiawa

Mana Pools National Park

Chiwore

Chewore Safari Area

▲ 1244m

Mata Pools

Urungwe Safari Area
(Campfire Eco-Tourism Area)

Angwa

Z A M B E Z I   E S C A R P M E N T

▲ 1020m

A1

50

MARINDA HILLS

Marongora

▲ 1239m

▲ 1288m

Makuti

GOTAGOTA HILLS

RAWAMOMBE RANGE

75

Doma Safari Area

Manyati

Charara Safari Area

Vuti

75

75

CHOUKA HILLS

Angwa

▲ 1336m

Mwami

▲ 1409m

40

WHAMIRA HILLS

30

20

15

Karoi

▲ 1360m

Mhangura

Magunge

▲ 1385m

15

Madadzi

45

Manyame

▲ 1242m

Deve

Msukwi

75

Zemaiwa

▲ 1267m

A1

▲ 1469m

HUNYANI RANGE

Fulechi

Chidamoyo

Chimusimbe

▲ 1278m

Sanyati

▲ 1202m

Mushowe

Zave

Lions Den

Mazwikadei Dam

Gandavaroyi Falls

ZANGOSE RANGE

CHEMBADZI HILLS

▲ 1356m

▲ 1369m

Eldorado

Dunphaile

Chiwi Rapids

Sanyati

Biriviri

Sangwe

Alaska

Chinhoyi

Banket

25

Machihiri

93

25

MEMBO HILLS

Greycourt

HARARE

Mupfure

▲ 913m

▲ 1016m

Trelawney

Argo

47

39

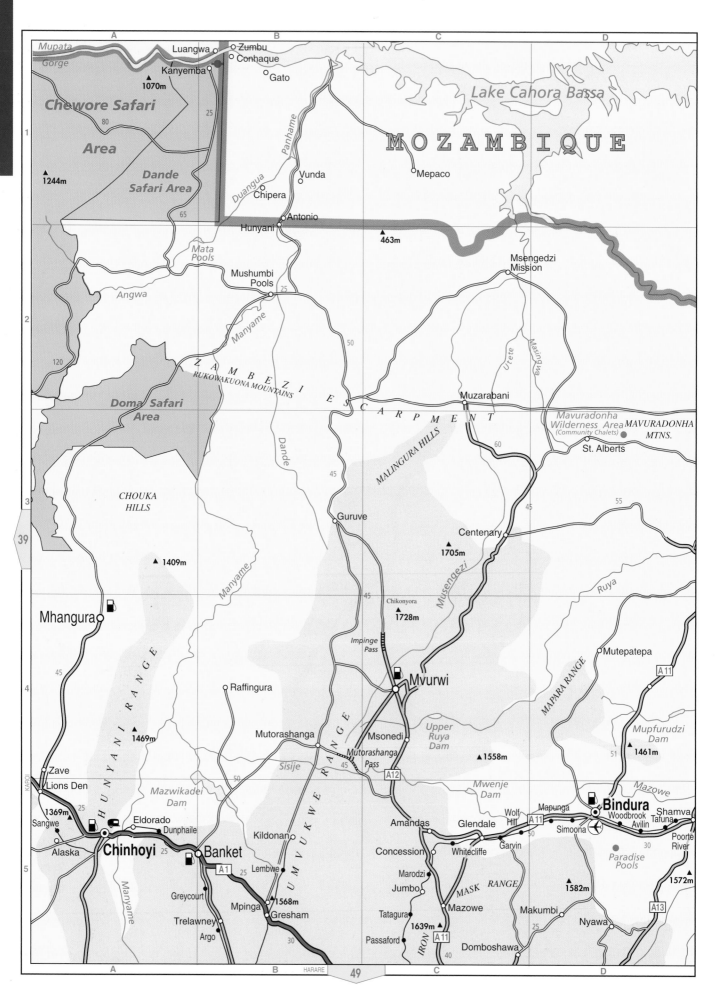

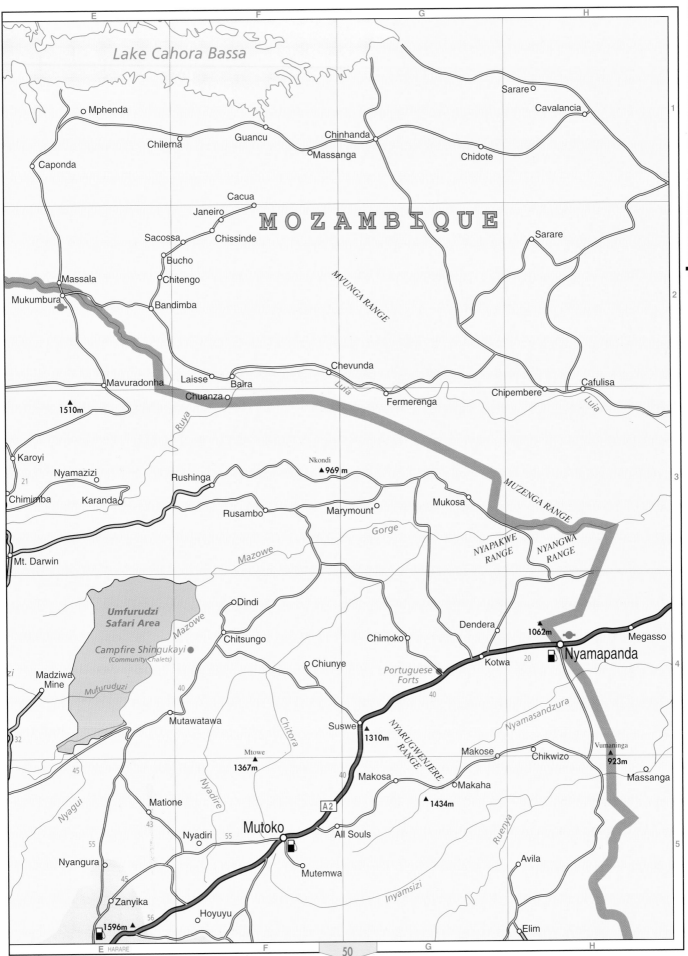

Lake Cahora Bassa

Mphenda
Chilerna
Guancu
Chinhanda
Massanga
Sarare
Cavalancia
Chidote
Caponda

M O Z A M B I Q U E

Cacua
Janeiro
Sacossa
Chissinde
Bucho
Chitengo
Massala
Bandimba
Mukumbura

Sarare

MVUNGA RANGE

Chevunda
Laisse
Baira
Mavuradonha
Chuanza
Luia
Fermerenga
Chipembere
Cafulisa
Luia

▲ 1510m

Ruya

Karoyi
Nyamazizi
Chimimba
Karanda
Rushinga
Nkondi
▲ 969 m
Mukosa
MUZENGA RANGE

21

Rusambo
Marymount
Gorge
NYAPAKWE RANGE
NYANGWA RANGE

Mazowe

Mt. Darwin

Umfurudzi
Safari Area
Dindi
Chimoko
Dendera
1062m
Megasso

Campfire Shingukayi ●
(Community Chalets)

Mazowe

Chitsungo
Chiunye
Portuguese
Forts
Kotwa
20
🅿 Nyamapanda

Madziwa
Mine

Mufuruduzi

40

Nyamasandzura

32

Mutawatawa
Suswe
▲ 1310m
NYARUGWENJERE RANGE
Makose
Chikwizo
Vumaninga
▲ 923m
Massanga

Chitora

45

Mtowe
▲
1367m

40

Makosa
Makaha
▲ 1434m

Nyadire

Matione

Nyagui

43

Mutoko
Nyadiri
55
A2
All Souls

Ruenya

Avila

55

Nyangura

45

Mutemwa

Inyamsizi

Zanyika
Hoyuyu

56

▲ 1596m ▲

Elim

Victoria Falls and Hwange

The Zambezi River, fourth largest of Africa's watercourses, rises in the well-watered Lunda uplands of Zambia, flowing south and then east to form the Zimbabwe-Zambia frontier, and at one point to plunge over the awesome Victoria Falls (see page 18). Downstream of the falls the river fills the great man-made lake of Kariba. Upstream is the eastern tip of Namibia's lush Caprivi region, the meeting point of four countries. The great grassland plains to the south are largely given over to safari areas, and to the preservation of wildlife, at its most prolific in Zimbabwe's largest game reserve, the magnificent Hwange National Park (see page 13).

There are no direct tarred land routes between Harare and the prime tourist destinations of Victoria Falls and Hwange National Park in the far northwest. Travellers can reach these areas via either Bulawayo on the A8, or Kariba.

Good roads also lead north to Livingstone and beyond, to Lusaka, the Zambian capital, and westwards to the Kazungula-Kasane area of Botswana.

Victoria Falls National Park The approaches to the falls and a narrow strip along the Zambezi's southern bank have been set aside as a 23km² (9 sq miles) park (*see* page 18). The area's principal feature is its rainforest, a magical place of fig and ebony, palm and sausage trees festooned with vines, lianas and ferns, the whole nurtured by drifting spray and the rich humus of the soil.

Here there are some fine viewpoints, one of them an observation platform cut into the side of the precipitous gorge close to the thundering Devil's Cataract.

You can also take in the falls from the Zambian side, and from the bridge linking the two countries (there are customs formalities, but they are minimal).

Zambezi National Park This 57,000ha (140,847 acres) conservation area, situated above the falls, extends southwards from the river. Abundant wildlife includes elephant, buffalo, giraffe, zebra, a diversity of antelope, lion, leopard and cheetah.

A circular game-viewing drive leads along the enchanting 46km (29 mile) river frontage and then through the southern sector. About 20 self-catering riverside lodges and several fishing camps have been established within the park's boundaries.

Hwange National Park Forming the largest part of the Hwange wildlife area, in the northwest corner of Zimbabwe, the park is considered to be one of Africa's greatest game sanctuaries.

The larger public camps are Main (*see* page 13), Sinamatella and Robins, each of

which has comfortable, fully equipped self-catering cottages and chalets, a fuel outlet, a grocery store that stocks basic provisions, and a limited number of caravan-camping stands (waterborne toilet facilities and ablutions). Main and Sinamatella each boast a restaurant and cocktail bar. Escorted walks are conducted from the three camps, and longer wilderness trails set out from Sinamatella and Robins. At Main Camp's waterhole you can watch the animals by moonlight – a magical experience.

Outside the park's boundaries are a number of private safari venues, each with its own personality and attractions. Notable are Sikumi Tree Lodge where the rooms, supported on stilts, are built into huge mangwe trees; the Sable Valley Lodge; Hwange Safari Lodge, a three-star hotel; Ivory Lodge offering tree houses, in a classic Out-of-Africa setting; and Jabulisa Camp, a converted farmstead with charming ethnic decor.

Kazuma Pan National Park The 31,300ha (77,342 acre) grassland reserve on the Botswana border is home to zebra, giraffe, buffalo, elephant and a variety of antelope. Its natural pans attract numerous waterbirds, especially kingfishers, cormorants, and the rare wattle crane.

There is no permanent accommodation and two rudimentary campsites, Insiza and Kasetsheti, provide the only facilities.

HWANGE	J	F	M	A	M	J	J	A	S	O	N	D
AVERAGE TEMP. °F	75	73	73	70	63	57	59	63	72	75	77	75
AVERAGE TEMP. °C	24	23	23	2	17	14	15	17	22	24	25	24
Hours of Sun Daily	8	8	8	9	9	9	10	11	11	9	9	7
RAINFALL ins.	6	5	3	1.5	0	0	0	0	0	1	2	6
RAINFALL mm	162	147	72	32	4	1	0	1	4	24	67	155
Days of Rainfall	16	14	9	4	1	0	0	0	1	4	10	15

Above: *The Victoria Falls plunge over the 1708m (5604ft) rim in a series of grand cataracts. The Falls are at their most spectacular in the months after the rains – between February and May.*
Below: *Sightseeing, by launch, above the Falls.*

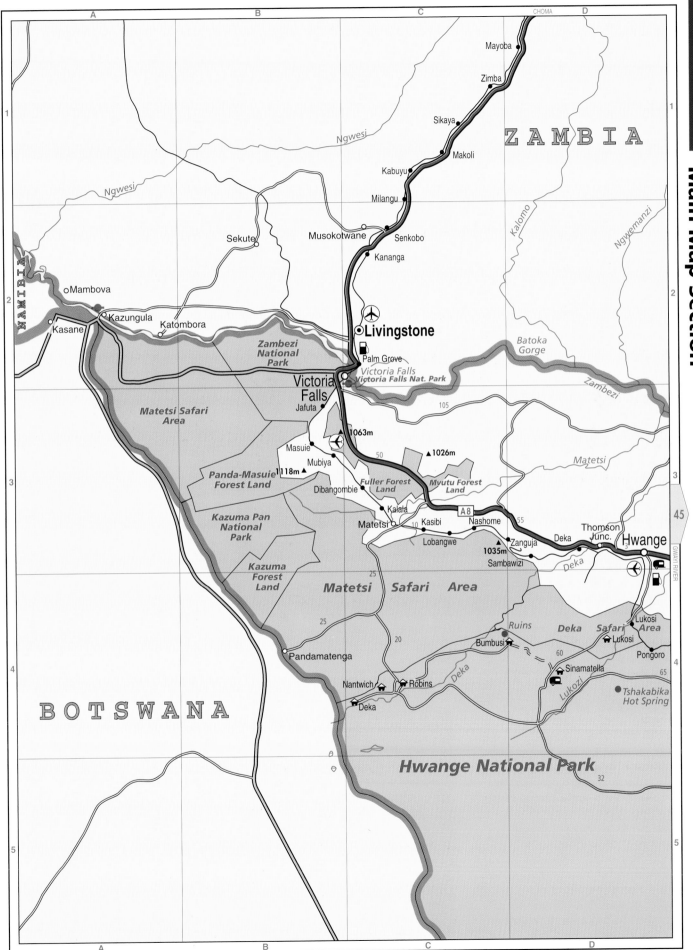

ZAMBIA

Mayoba

Zimba

Sikaya

Makoli

Kabuyu

Milangu

Senkobo

Musokotwane

Kananga

Sekute

NAMIBIA

Mambova

Kazungula

Kasane

Katombora

Livingstone

Batoka Gorge

Zambezi National Park

Palm Grove

Victoria Falls

Victoria Falls Nat. Park

Zambezi

Matetsi Safari Area

Jafuta

▲1063m

▲1026m

Matetsi

105

50

Masuie

Mubiya

118m ▲

Panda-Masuie Forest Land

Fuller Forest Land

Mvutu Forest Land

Dibangombie

Kalala

A8

55

Kazuma Pan National Park

Matetsi

Kasibi

Nashome

Deka

Thomson Junc.

Hwange

10

45

Kazuma Forest Land

Lobangwe

Zanguja

3

▲1035m

Sambawizi

Deka

Matetsi Safari Area

25

Lukosi Area

Ruins

Deka

Safari

Lukosi

20

Bumbusi

Pongoro

25

Sinamatella

65

Pandamatenga

60

BOTSWANA

Nantwich

Robins

Deka

Tshakabika Hot Spring

Deka

Lukozi

Hwange National Park

32

GWAYI RIVER

CHOMA

Ngwesi

Ngwesi

Kalomo

Ngwemanzi

Western Kariba

The upper reaches of Lake Kariba are less developed for tourism than the area around Kariba town and the dam wall at the northeastern end. Discerning fishermen, however, favour the comparative solitude of the western waters and the broad stretch of the Zambezi to the east of Hwange. They invariably record impressive catches of bream and, especially, the sporting tigerfish. Game-viewers are also drawn to the region: Chete, the lake's largest island, and its adjacent safari area are renowned for their elephant herds, the Chizarira hills invite exploration, and, of course, there are the splendours of the Hwange National Park not too far away.

Untarred roads are the only means of accessing the area south of Lake Kariba, though the ferry is a rewarding way of travelling the length of the lake while, at the same time, taking in some memorable sightseeing and game-viewing.

Two largish car-ferries ply the 282km (175 mile) route between Mlibizi at the southwestern end and Kariba's busiest harbour, Andora, near Kariba town and the dam wall to the northeast.

Chizarira National Park

This 1910 km² (738 sq mile) conservation area extends over the rugged Chizarira Hills of the escarpment to the south of the lake – a wild and remote area accessible only by four-wheel-drive vehicles.

Here there are small exclusive camps, and also the privately run Chizarira Wilderness Safari Lodge, whose comfortable chalets, perched dramatically at the edge of a cliff, afford breathtaking views across the bush to the distant waters.

The wildlife complement includes elephant, buffalo, sable, tsessebe and roan antelope. On offer are escorted day-long bush walks and wilderness trails.

Binga The centre of the lake's western segment is Binga. It comprises a scatter of buildings, set on a modest range of hills,

that includes an excellent rest-camp, with its hot-spring-fed pool, the fully equipped Chilila and Kulizwe lodges, and some lakeside holiday homes. It also offers camping stands for caravans, a restaurant, bar, supermarket, post office, fuel outlet, and a small fishing harbour. The nearby crocodile farm is worth a visit.

Mlibizi The harbour of Mlibizi, on Kariba's southwestern shore, serves as a terminus for the ferries, and is similar to, but smaller than, Binga. Here, close to the striking formations of the Sebungwe Narrows, where Zimbabwean and Zambian shores are a mere 200m (656ft) apart, there are located a rest-camp, which offers comfortable chalets, a campsite, restaurant, shop and two swimming pools. Rafts and boats are also available for hire.

Hwange Located on the main highway 50km (31 miles) south of Victoria Falls, the town of Hwange lies outside the boundaries of the national park but offers access to one of its main camps, Sinamatella, and to the Deka Safari Area.

It draws its prosperity from extensive coal-mining operations, and the highlight of a visit to the town is to see the steam locomotives that puff along the region's rail network. The town's Baobab Hotel is a good place to stop for refreshments, a meal and for superb views over Hwange National Park (see page 13) to the southwest.

KARIBA SOUTH	J	F	M	A	M	J	J	A	S	O	N	D
AVERAGE TEMP. °F	77	77	77	77	73	68	68	73	79	79	81	79
AVERAGE TEMP. °C	25	25	25	25	23	20	20	23	26	26	27	26
Hours of Sun Daily	7	7	8	9	9	9	10	10	10	10	10	6
RAINFALL ins.	67	68	35	13	2	2	0	0	0	0	5	7
RAINFALL mm	171	172	89	32	5	5	0	1	1	1	13	18
Days of Rainfall	14	14	8	4	1	1	0	0	0	0	2	13

Above left: *The Kariba ferry provides both transport and a memorable means of seeing the lake. The voyage between Andora harbour and Mlibizi takes 22 hours, and the vessel offers comfortable saloon chairs and full bar facilities.*
Left: *The regal lion, a prominent resident of Hwange and the Zambezi wildlife areas. The male tends to be indolent, but is immensely powerful and can show a remarkable turn of speed.*

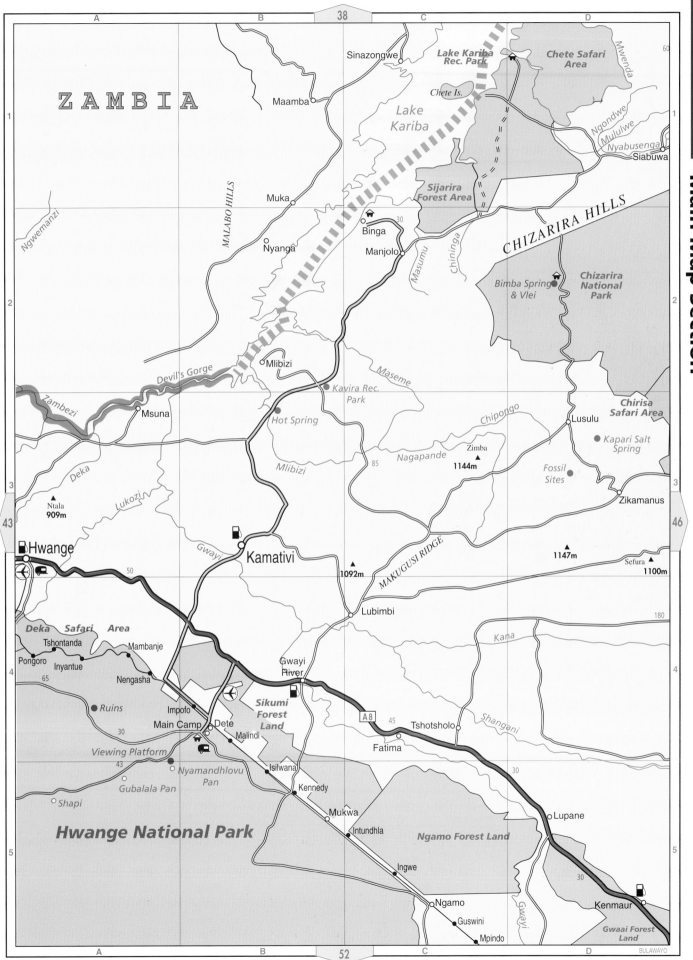

38

43

46

52

ZAMBIA

Sinazongwe

Maamba

Muka

Nyanga

MALABO HILLS

Ngwemanzi

Lake Kariba
Rec. Park

Chete Is.

Lake
Kariba

Chete Safari
Area

Mwenda

Ngondwe

Mululwe

Nyabusenga

Siabuwa

Binga

Manjolo

Sijarira
Forest Area

Masumu

Chininga

CHIZARIRA HILLS

Bimba Spring
& Vlei

Chizarira
National
Park

Mlibizi

Devil's Gorge

Zambezi

Msuna

Deka

Lukozi

Ntala
909m

Hot Spring

Mlibizi

Kavira Rec.
Park

Maseme

Nagapande

Chipongo

Zimba
1144m

Fossil
Sites

Lusulu

Chirisa
Safari Area

Kapari Salt
Spring

Zikamanus

Gwayi

Kamativi

1092m

MAKUGUSI RIDGE

1147m

Sefura
1100m

Hwange

50

Lubimbi

Kana

180

Deka Safari Area

Tshontanda

Pongoro

Inyantue

Mambanje

Nengasha

65

Ruins

Impofo

Main Camp

Dete

30

Viewing Platform

43

Gubalala Pan

Shapi

Nyamandhlovu
Pan

Sikumi
Forest
Land

Malindi

Isilwana

Kennedy

Gwayi
River

Shangani

A8

45

Tshotsholo

Fatima

30

Hwange National Park

Mukwa

Intundhla

Ngamo Forest Land

Lupane

Ingwe

30

Ngamo

Guswini

Gwayi

Kenmaur

Gwaai Forest
Land

Mpindo

BULAWAYO

60

1

1

2

2

3

3

4

4

5

5

A

B

C

D

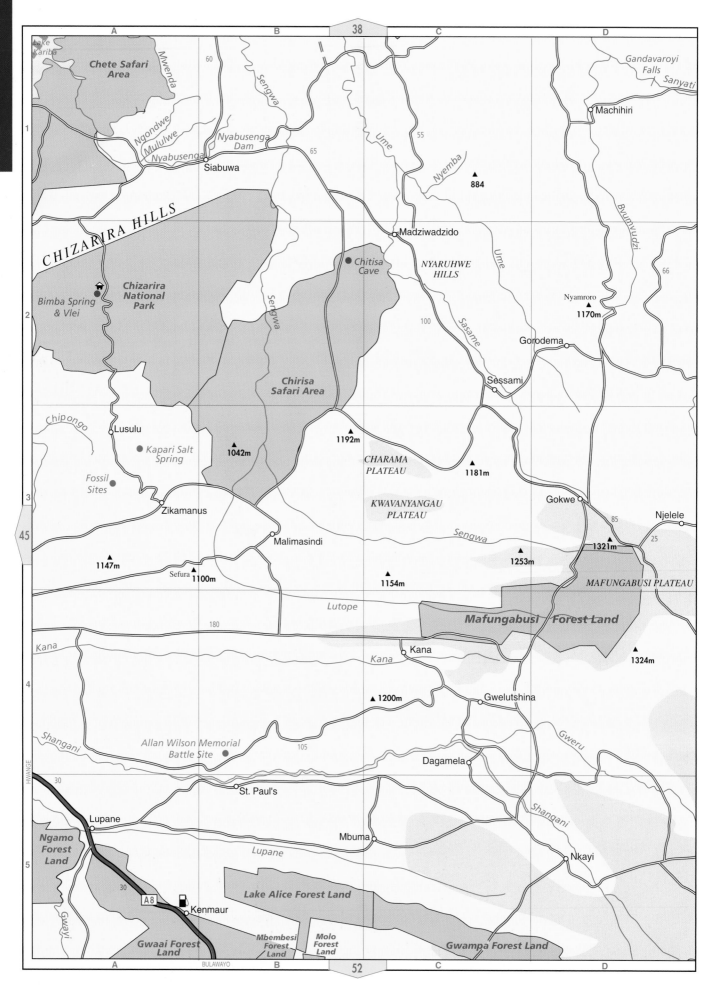

Lake
Kariba

Chete Safari Area

60

Mwenda

Ngondwe

Mululwe

Nyabusenga

Nyabusenga Dam

Siabuwa

65

Sengwa

Ume

55

Nyemba

▲
884

Machihiri

Gandavaroyi Falls

Sanyati

Bvumvudzi

66

CHIZARIRA HILLS

Madziwadzido

Chitisa Cave

NYARUHWE HILLS

Ume

Sasame

100

Nyamroro
▲
1170m

Gorodema

Chizarira National Park

🏠
Bimba Spring & Vlei

Sessami

Chipongo

Lusulu

Chirisa Safari Area

Sengwa

Kapari Salt Spring

▲
1042m

▲
1192m

CHARAMA PLATEAU

▲
1181m

Gokwe

Njelele

85

25

Fossil Sites

KWAVANYANGAU PLATEAU

Sengwa

▲
1253m

▲
1321m

MAFUNGABUSI PLATEAU

Zikamanus

Malimasindi

▲
1147m

Sefura ▲
1100m

▲
1154m

Lutope

180

Mafungabusi Forest Land

▲
1324m

Kana

Kana

Kana

▲ **1200m**

Gwelutshina

Gweru

Shangani

Allan Wilson Memorial Battle Site

105

Dagamela

HWANGE

30

St. Paul's

Lupane

Ngamo Forest Land

30

A8

🚏
Kenmaur

Mbuma

Lupane

Shangani

Nkayi

Lake Alice Forest Land

Gwaai Forest Land

Mbembesi Forest Land

Molo Forest Land

Gwampa Forest Land

Gwayi

BULAWAYO

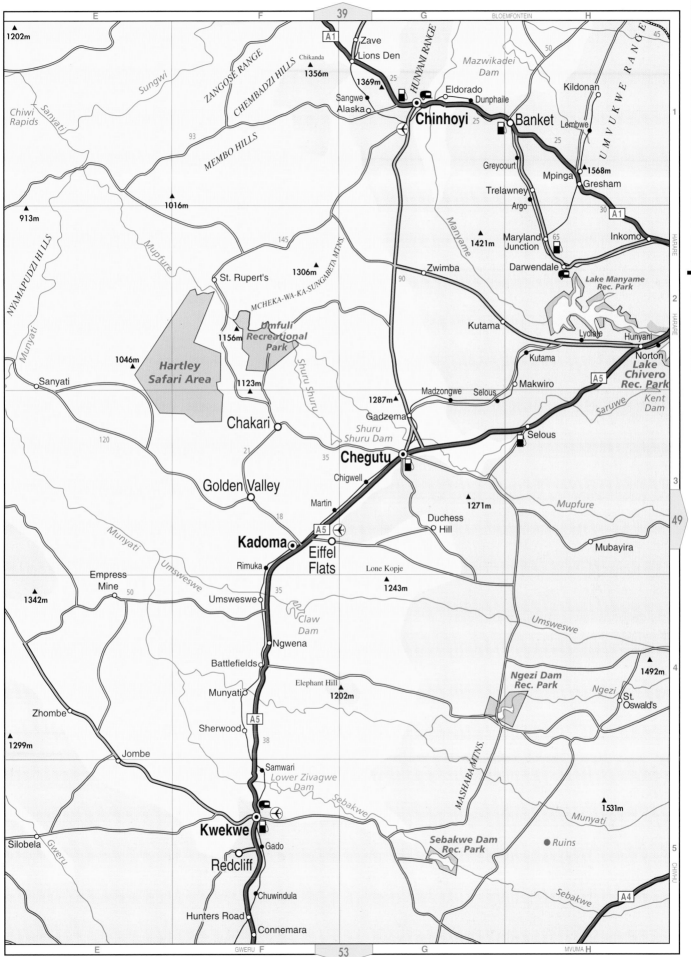

Main Map Section

1202m

ZANGOSÉ RANGE
CHEMBADZI HILLS
Chikanda
1356m

Sungwi
Sanyati
Chiwi
Rapids

MEMBO HILLS
93

1016m

913m

NYAMAPUDZI HILLS

Mupfure
Munyati

A1
Zave
Lions Den
HUNYANI RANGE
BLOEMFONTEIN

50
45

1369m
Sangwe
Alaska
25

Chinhoyi
25

Eldorado
Dunphaile

Banket

Mazwikadei
Dam

Kildonan

Lembwe

UMVUKWE RANGE

Greycourt
Mpinga
Gresham
1568m

Trelawney
Argo
30
A1

1421m
Maryland
Junction
65
Inkomo

HARARE

Darwendale

Lake Manyame
Rec. Park

145

St. Rupert's

1306m

MCHEKA-WA-KA-SUNGABETA MTNS.

1156m
Umfuli
Recreational
Park

1046m

**Hartley
Safari Area**

1123m

Shuru Shuru

Sanyati

120

Chakari

Golden Valley

21

35

90

Zwimba

Kutama

Kutama

Madzongwe
Selous
Makwiro

1287m
Gadzema

Shuru
Shuru Dam

Chegutu

Chigwell

Selous

A5

Lydiate
Hunyani

Norton
**Lake
Chivero
Rec. Park**

Kent
Dam

Saruwe

Mupfure

HARARE

Martin

18

A5

Kadoma
Rimuka

**Eiffel
Flats**

1271m

Duchess
Hill

Lone Kopje

1243m

Mubayira

Empress
Mine
50

1342m

Umsweswe
35

Claw
Dam

Ngwena

Umsweswe

Munyati
Umsweswe

Battlefields

Munyati

Elephant Hill
1202m

A5

Sherwood

38

Ngezi Dam
Rec. Park

Ngezi
St.
Oswald's

1492m

Zhombe

1299m

Jombe

Samwari
Lower Zivagwe
Dam

Sebakwe

MASHABA MTNS.

1531m

Munyati

Silobela

Gweru

Kwekwe

Gado

Redcliff

Chuwindula

**Sebakwe Dam
Rec. Park**

Ruins

Sebakwe
A4
CHIVHU

Hunters Road

Connemara

GWERU
53
MVUMA

Harare Region

Zimbabwe's capital city and largest urban concentration is Harare, located 1470m (4823ft) above sea level in the northeastern segment of the country. Altitude and latitude – it lies north of the Tropic of Capricorn – combine to produce a superb climate: the highveld air is rare and heady, the hours filled with sunshine. Winters are bone dry, the skies clear, the days mild, the nights cold, and in the summer months the heat is invariably relieved by late afternoon downpours of heroic proportions. The surrounding countryside is flattish, fertile, attractive, largely given over to cattle, maize, tobacco, vegetables, citrus and other fruit.

Excellent tarred roads radiate from Harare, linking the city to Bulawayo (440km, 273 miles), Plumtree and the Botswana border (540km, 336 miles) in the southwest; Masvingo (290km, 180 miles), Beitbridge and the South African border (580km, 360 miles) in the south; Mutare (265km, 165 miles) and the Mozambique border in the east; and Kariba, Chirundu (350km, 217 miles) and the Zambian border in the remote northwest.

To reach the prime tourist destinations of Victoria Falls and Hwange National Park in the northwest, travellers have to go via either Bulawayo or Kariba because there are no direct tarred land routes.

The Kopje The prominent boulder-strewn, green-garlanded hillock or *Kopje* on the capital's southwestern fringes marks the point beneath which Cecil Rhodes' founding settlers encamped in September 1890 to inaugurate the colonial era.

The summit offers panoramic views of the city and surrounding countryside and a toposcope displays the directions and distances to places of interest.

Lake Chivero Recreational Park
To the southwest of Harare is the nature sanctuary and weekend resort of Lake Chivero Recreational Park (*see* page 9).

Visitors to the park can see wildlife, including kudu, reedbuck, baboon, monkey,

and such reintroduced species as giraffe, white rhino, wildebeest, eland and ostrich. The lake offers yachting and power-boating, and the park has a tea garden, hotel, caravan-camping sites, and National Parks lodges including the thatched Fish Eagle, Kingfisher and Mocking Chat.

Farther west is the less developed Lake Manyame Recreational Park, the centrepiece of which is the 81km² (31 sq mile) lake created by damming the Manyame River.

Mazowe The Mazowe Valley, 40km (25 miles) north of Harare, is the country's largest citrus area and a quite lovely day-drive destination. The local hotel is Zimbabwe's second oldest.

Marondera Situated on the Mutare road 74 km (46 miles) east of Harare, the town of Marondera is the attractive centre of an especially productive farming region embracing beef and dairy cattle pastures, tobacco lands, timber plantations, cornfields and vineyards (the region pioneered Zimbabwe's fledgling and promising wine industry). The town is also notable for its charming little racecourse.

Chinhoyi Also a flourishing agricultural town, specializing in cattle, maize, and tobacco, and a busy mining centre producing copper and chrome, it is Chinhoyi's magical caves that attract tourists.

The focus of a recreational area, the labyrinthine complex is actually a giant sinkhole – with a system of supplementary passages and chambers – filled with clear, intensely blue, iridescent water.

The African name for the caves is *Chirorodziva*, or 'place of the fallen', a reference to a grisly episode in the 1830s when many of the local inhabitants were hurled down to their deaths by raiding tribesmen.

Satellite safari lodges Within a 100km (62 miles) radius of Harare's city centre there is a number of private game reserves and lodges, each offering wildlife viewing and luxurious accommodation.

These include Landela and Imire Game reserves, both on the Mutare Road, and Mwanga Lodge in the Bally Vaughan Game Park on the Shamva Road.

Pamuzinda, set among shade trees beside the quiet Saruwe River, is situated near the small centre of Selous off the Bulawayo road (A5). The extensive estate provides sanctuary for a variety of wild animals, including several endangered species.

Below left: *The deep caves of Chinhoyi embrace a pool of magical beauty – and hide a gruesome past.*
Below: *Elephant and an ostrich make themselves at home in the grounds of the privately owned Pamuzinda Safari Lodge. Pamuzinda has 11 beautifully appointed double units, a 'royal suite' and an inviting central complex of dining and bar areas.*

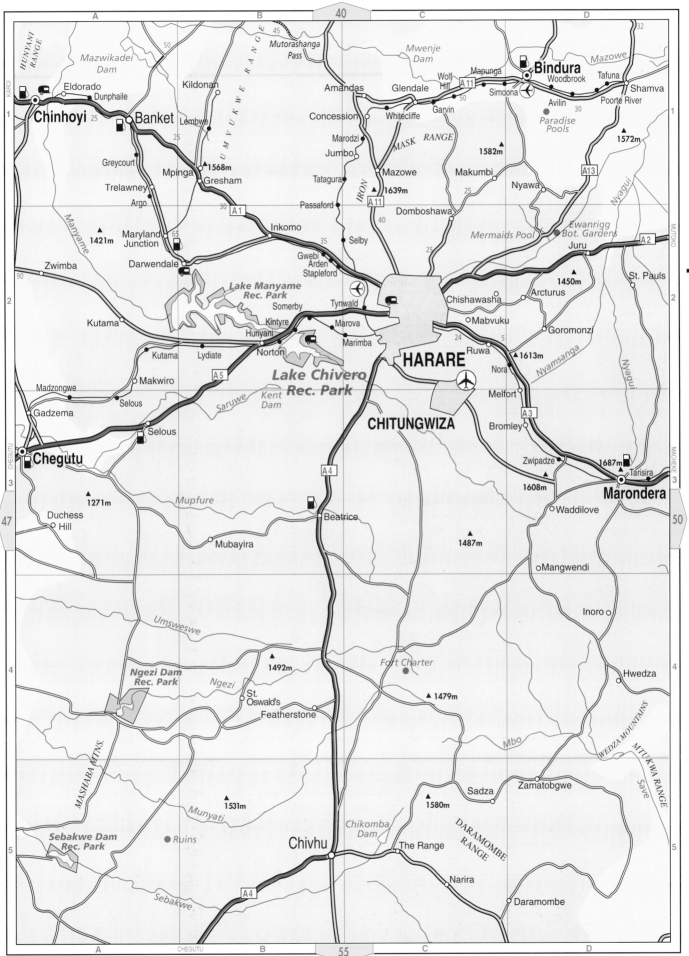

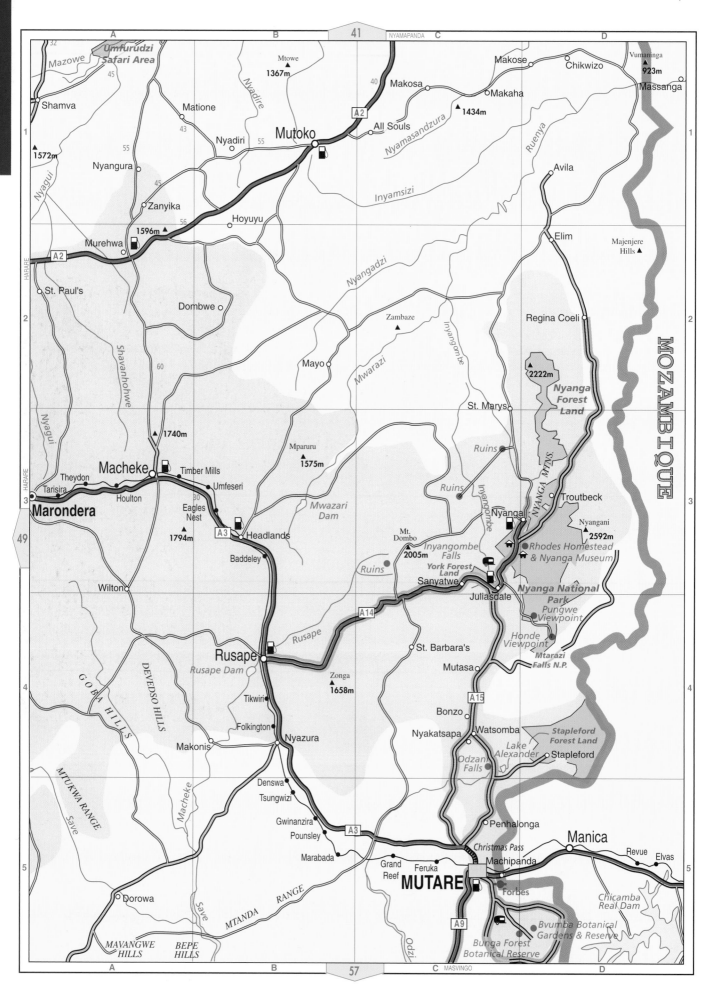

NYAMAPANDA

A   B   C   D

Umfurudzi Safari Area

Mazowe   32
45

Shamva   Matione   Mtowe
1367m
Makose   Chikwizo   Vumaninga
923m
Makosa   Massanga
▲ 1572m   Nyadiri   Mutoko   55   All Souls   Makaha   ▲ 1434m
Nyangura   Makaha
Zanyika   Hoyuyu   Avila
1596m ▲   56
Murehwa   Elim   Majenjere Hills ▲
A2
St. Paul's   Regina Coeli
Dombwe   Zambaze   ▲ 2222m   Nyanga Forest Land
Mayo   St. Marys
▲ 1740m   Mparuru
1575m   Ruins   Troutbeck
Macheke   Timber Mills   Ruins   Nyanga   Nyangani ▲ 2592m
Theydon   Umfeseri   Mt. Dombo   Rhodes Homestead & Nyanga Museum
Tarisira   Houlton   ▲ 2005m   Inyangombe Falls
Marondera   Eagles Nest   York Forest Land   Nyanga National Park
▲ 1794m   Headlands   Sanyatwe   Pungwe Viewpoint
Baddeley   Ruins   Juliasdale   Honde Viewpoint
Wilton   A14   Mtarazi Falls N.P.
Rusape   St. Barbara's   Mutasa
Rusape Dam   Bonzo   A15
Tikwiri   Zonga ▲ 1658m   Nyakatsapa   Watsomba   Stapleford Forest Land
Folkington   Odzani Falls   Lake Alexander   Stapleford
Makonis   Nyazura
Denswa   Penhalonga   Manica
Tsungwizi   Revue   Elvas
Gwinanzira   A3   Christmas Pass   Machipanda
Pounsley   Grand Reef   Feruka   MUTARE   Forbes
Marabada   A9
Dorowa   Bvumba Botanical Gardens & Reserve
MAVANGWE HILLS   BEPE HILLS   Bunga Forest Botanical Reserve   Chicamba Real Dam

MOZAMBIQUE

HARARE   A2
HARARE

GOBA HILLS   DEVEDSO HILLS

MTUKWA RANGE   Save   Macheke   Save   MTANDA RANGE

Bulawayo Region

The southwestern part of Zimbabwe covers part of the Midlands province and much of the so-called Middleveld (see pages 52 and 53), a region lying between 600 and 1200m (1968-3937ft) above sea level. Here it is warmer, drier and generally less fertile than the highveld plateau to the north and often afflicted by savage drought, but nevertheless extensively farmed and ranched. Bulawayo, the main urban centre, is a city of about half a million people, most of them of Ndebele stock. The settlement was founded in 1872, as guBulawayo – which means 'the place of slaughter' – by the Ndebele king Lobengula.

From Bulawayo well-maintained highways run to Harare (440km, 273 miles) in the northeast, and east to and then along the Chimanimani and Bvumba highlands as far as Mutare (580km, 360 miles) and the Mozambique border.

The A6 stretches south to Beitbridge (320km, 199 miles) and the South African border while the A7 leads to Plumtree (100km, 62 miles) and the Botswana border to the southwest. Hwange National Park and Victoria Falls (440km, 273 miles) to the northwest are accessible via the A8 (*see page 42*).

Hillside Dam Nature Reserve
Just to the south of Bulawayo, the Hillside Dam Nature Reserve is a delightful compound of lake, lawn and granite outcrop that incorporates picnic spots, a tea room and aviary. It is a lovely place for rambles.

Chipangali Wildlife Orphanage
Animal lovers can visit Chipangali Wildlife Orphanage situated 23km (14 miles) from the city centre on the A6 – the Beitbridge Road. It takes in and cares for sick, injured and abandoned animals and birds, and whenever possible returns them to the wild. It is also a centre for a duiker conservation project.

Cyrene Mission
Southwest of Bulawayo, on the A7, is the Cyrene Mission, an Anglican church mission founded as an educational centre for African children. It is now noted for its arts and crafts, especially sculpture, carving, and painting representing both traditional and religious subjects.

Matobo Hills and National Park
The area to the south of Bulawayo – Matobo Hills and the associated National Park – is famed for its rugged granite formations, caves which contain Bushman paintings, wildlife, black eagles, and viewpoints such as World's View, the site of Cecil Rhodes' grave (*see page 16*).

Kame Ruins
The renowned ruins were once the headquarters of a powerful ancestral

Shona dynasty (of the Rosvi empire), later serving as a sacred Ndebele shrine.

The ruins, scattered over a fairly wide area, are a World Heritage Site, though they were severely damaged by European intruders after their 'discovery' in 1893. There is a small site museum.

Nalatale Ruins
Southwest of Gweru is the ancient ruined settlement of Nalatale. The architecturally impressive stone structures are decorated with intricate chevron, herringbone and chequer patterns.

Other important ruined sites in the area include the Regina Complex and Dhlo Dhlo, or Danangombe, both of which have yielded gold and other artefacts.

Gweru
Capital of the Midlands province and fourth largest of Zimbabwe's urban centres, Gweru has a solid industrial base. Among local attractions are the Midlands Museum, the National Military Museum, and the Antelope Game Park.

Kwekwe
Among the drawcards of Kwekwe, situated to the north of Gweru, is the National Gold Mining Museum, whose unusual centrepiece is a 'paper house'. The prefabricated structure, made from papier-

Top: *The craggy grandeur of the Matobo Hills, to the south of Bulawayo. The high cliffs provide eyries for the world's largest concentration of the handsome black eagle.*
Above: *The walls of the Nalatale Ruins, intricately patterned in chequer, chevron and herringbone, are among the country's most attractive archaeological sites.*

mâché panels, cardboard and wood, was home to an early mine manager.

The name Kwekwe is said to be derived from the word used to describe the night-time symphony of frogs that inhabit the local river.

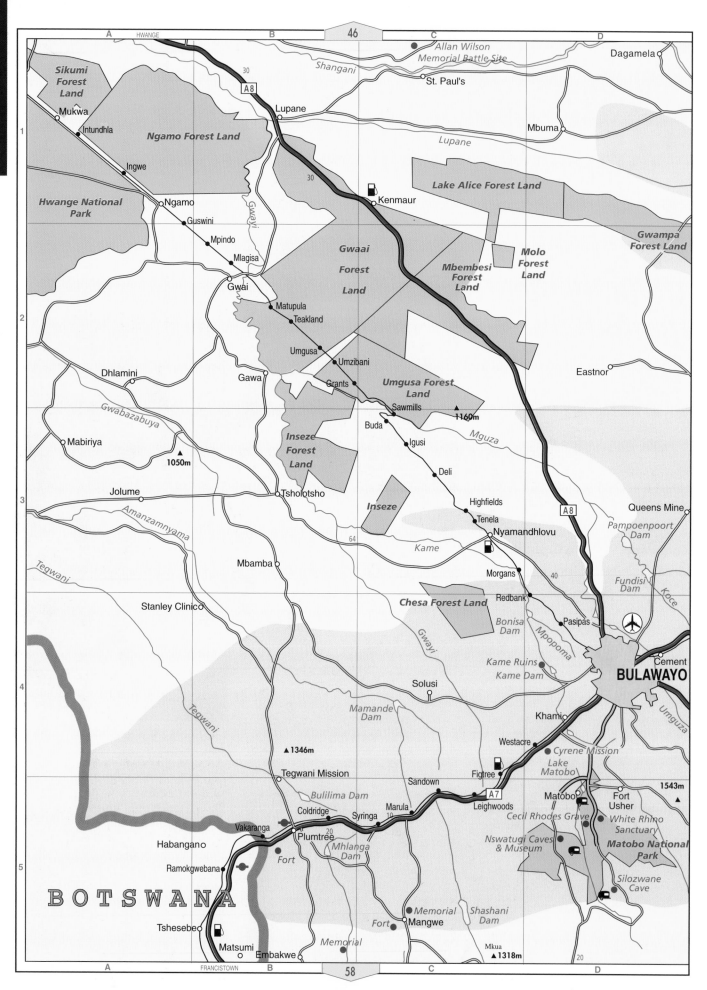

A · B · C · D

Sikumi
Forest
Land

Mukwa

Intundhla

Ngamo Forest Land

A8

30

Lupane

Shangani

Allan Wilson
Memorial Battle Site

St. Paul's

Dagamela

Mbuma

Lupane

Ingwe

Hwange National
Park

Ngamo

Guswini

Mpindo

Mlagisa

Gwai

30

Kenmaur

Lake Alice Forest Land

Gwaai
Forest
Land

Mbembesi
Forest
Land

Molo
Forest
Land

Gwampa
Forest Land

Matupula

Teakland

Umgusa

Umzibani

Eastnor

Dhlamini

Gawa

Grants

Gwabazabuya

Umgusa Forest
Land

Sawmills

1160m

Mguza

Mabiriya

1050m

Inseze
Forest
Land

Buda

Igusi

Deli

Jolume

Tsholotsho

Inseze

Highfields

Tenela

Nyamandhlovu

A8

Queens Mine

Pampoenpoort
Dam

Amanzamnyama

64

Kame

Morgans

40

Fundisi
Dam

Koce

Mbamba

Chesa Forest Land

Redbank

Pasipas

Tegwani

Stanley Clinico

Gwayi

Bonisa
Dam

Mpopoma

Cement

Kame Ruins

Kame Dam

BULAWAYO

Umguza

Tegwani

Mamande
Dam

Solusi

Khamic

1346m

Westacre

Cyrene Mission

Lake
Matobo

1543m

Tegwani Mission

Sandown

Figtree

Matobo

Fort
Usher

Bulilima Dam

Coldridge

Syringa

Marula

10

A7

Leighwoods

Cecil Rhodes Grave

White Rhino
Sanctuary

Matobo National
Park

Vakaranga

Plumtree

Nswatugi Caves
& Museum

Habangano

20

Mhlanga
Dam

Fort

Silozwane
Cave

Ramokgwebana

BOTSWANA

Memorial

Fort

Memorial

Mangwe

Shashani
Dam

Tshesebe

Matsumi

Embakwe

Memorial

Mkua

1318m

20

A · B · C · D

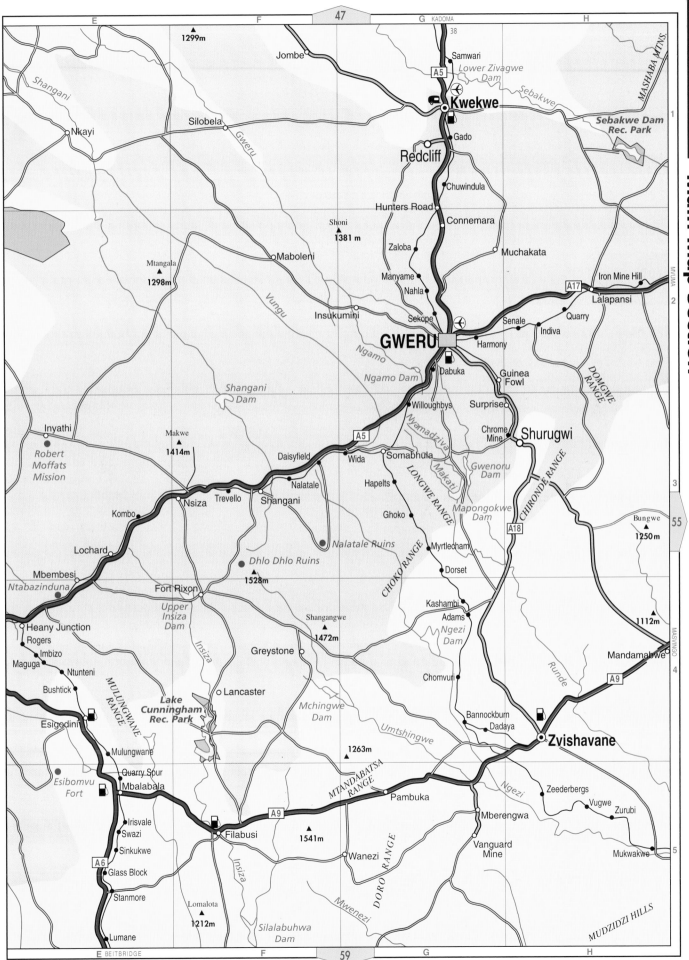

Masvingo Area

Masvingo, known as Fort Victoria in the colonial days, is Zimbabwe's oldest town. It began life as a fortified encampment built by Cecil Rhodes' intrusive Pioneer Column on its way north in August 1890. Today it is a largish place – it has five hotels and some lovely suburban gardens – that functions as the capital of the Masvingo province, a region whose prosperity derives from farming (maize, tobacco), ranching, mining and tourism. Not too far away to the east and south lie the inviting waters of Lake Mutirikwi Recreational Area and the ruins of Great Zimbabwe, one of the country's premier attractions (see page 32).

The A4 links Masvingo with Beitbridge (290km, 180 miles) at the South African border in the south, and the same road extends northwards leading to the capital, Harare (290km, 180 miles).

Chimanimani (280km, 174 miles) and Mutare (295km, 183 miles) on the Mozambique border are accessible via the A9.

Lake Mutirikwi Formerly known as Lake Kyle, Lake Mutirikwi is Zimbabwe's third largest expanse of water and the focus of a fairly well-developed recreational area and game reserve.

The 63m (207ft) high dam wall and 92km² (36 sq miles) lake was created to feed the huge lowveld sugar and citrus estates to the southeast. The Masvingo region has suffered badly from drought (the lake dried up completely in the early 1990s) but has an impressive capacity for recovery.

Animals introduced into the park's game reserve, located along the lake's northern shores, include white rhino, giraffe and a number of antelope, and bird species, including the rock thrush, collared sunbird, and the lanner falcon, often seen near the Great Zimbabwe ruins. Hippo wallow and crocodile bask in the shallows.

Visitor amenities comprise self-contained lodges, caravan and camping sites, picnic spots, mooring sites for boats. Game-viewing walks and facilities for fishing are also offered.

Manjirenji and Bangala recreational parks

Southeast of Masvingo are two recreational parks, Bangala and Manjirenji. The focus of the latter is Lake Manjirenji which is popular for the excellent fishing and boating that it offers, and for its scenery.

Sebakwe Dam Recreational Park

Situated about 39km (24 miles) east of Kwekwe (see page 53), Sebakwe Dam Recreational Park sustains kudu, impala and an interesting variety of waterbirds.

The park's main attractions are fishing and nature walks, and there are campsites, overnight cottages and a caravan park.

Mushandike Sanctuary The Mushandike Sanctuary, some 30km (19 miles) west of Masvingo, is a multi-purpose area that combines game-farming, wildlife conservation, recreation, research and education. Among the animals that can be seen are white rhino, zebra, antelope, klipspringer, wildebeest and leopard.

The hill-girded dam is popular among anglers for its black bass, tilapia and bream.

Top: *Lake Mutirikwi, to the northeast of Great Zimbabwe, is the country's third largest reservoir.*
Left: *Giraffe are numbered among the Mutirikwi park's large game. The lake itself sustains, among other wildlife, hippo and crocodile.*
Above: *A selection of locally crafted pots.*

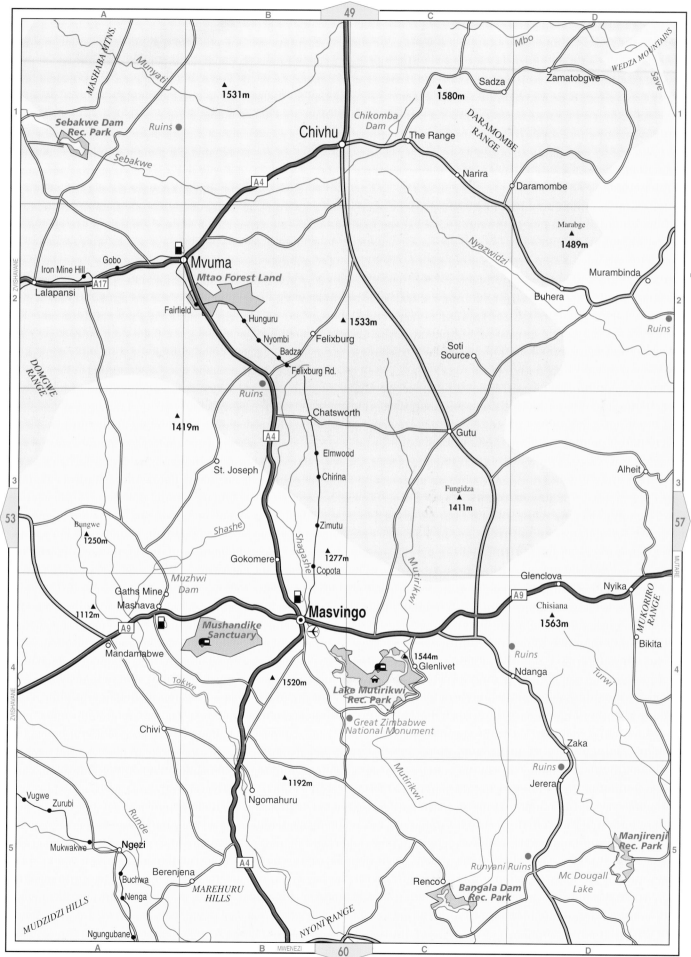

Eastern Highlands

The southern section of the Eastern Highlands is a scenically stunning region – of remote valleys and tree-mantled hills, mountain streams, waterfalls and pools – that embraces the famed Chimanimani National Park. Its northern gateway is the city of Mutare, its southern the pretty little village of Chipinge. To reach the latter you cross the Save River, a major watercourse that rises on the highveld plateau 100km (62 miles) from Harare to flow south-wards, helping irrigate the splendid Lowveld citrus and sugar estates before entering Mozambique on its way to the Indian Ocean.

The three principal routes to the region are fully tarred and well maintained. The northern one (A3) leads from Harare to Mutare, a distance of 265km (165 miles).

Visitors entering Zimbabwe at the southern border post of Beitbridge, however, can turn off to the right either at Ngundu and drive east on the A10 to and through the Lowveld town of Chiredzi, or at Masvingo, following the A9 to and across the Save River via the Birchenough Bridge.

Mutare Zimbabwe's fourth largest city, Mutare, is situated amid the grand mountains of Zimbabwe's eastern rampart. The town is attractively laid out, its quiet streets graced by a profusion of flowering trees that are at their most colourful in springtime.

The history of the city and the surrounding highlands is displayed at the Mutare Museum. On Murahwa's Hill visitors can see Iron Age ruins, and the Mutare Heights Road offers the best views of the city. There are four good hotels and a caravan park.

Chimanimani National Park

Chimanimani National Park (*see page 30*) occupies just over 171km² (66 sq miles) of mist-wreathed upland terrain graced by natural forest, heath, grassland and a wild flower extravaganza that includes proteas, ericas and everlastings.

This is primarily walking (and trout fishing) country; there are no internal roads except that which leads to the base camp. The village of Chimanimani has a hotel and a caravan-camping ground.

Birchenough Bridge Travellers bound for the Eastern Highlands on the route through Masvingo cross the Save River via the impressive Birchenough Bridge.

It was built in 1935 and at that time ranked as the world's third largest suspension bridge. Apart from the difference in size, it is an exact replica of the larger and more famous Sydney harbour bridge.

Chimanimani Village A delightful little centre that enjoys a wonderfully temperate climate, Chimanimani village receives plenty of sun but, because of its altitude – it lies 1588m (5210ft) above sea level – the weather is rarely too hot for comfort.

The wider area, inhabited for the most part by the Vendao people, encompasses a number of ancient ruins similar to but much smaller than Great Zimbabwe (*see page 32*). There are also some impressive Bushman rock-art sites, most notably around the old drift across the Save River.

Chipinge Southeast of Birchenough Bridge lies the Chimanimani region's main town and centre, Chipinge.

Recommended is a visit to the Chirinda Forest Botanical Reserve, near Mount Selinda, whose Valley of the Giants sustains (among others) hundreds of rare, huge and venerable red mahogany trees.

MUTARE	J	F	M	A	M	J	J	A	S	O	N	D
AVERAGE TEMP. °F	73	70	68	68	63	57	57	61	63	66	70	73
AVERAGE TEMP. °C	23	21	20	20	17	14	14	16	17	19	21	23
Hours of Sun Daily	6	6	7	8	8	8	8	9	9	9	7	6
RAINFALL ins.	65	61	33	11	5	3	2	3	8	16	36	65
RAINFALL mm	165	157	86	28	13	8	5	7	20	41	92	165
Days of Rainfall	13	13	9	8	2	2	2	2	2	5	9	12

Above left: *Mount Selinda's often misty evergreen forest.*
Below: *The huge span of the Birchenough Bridge, western gateway to the Chimanimani mountains.*

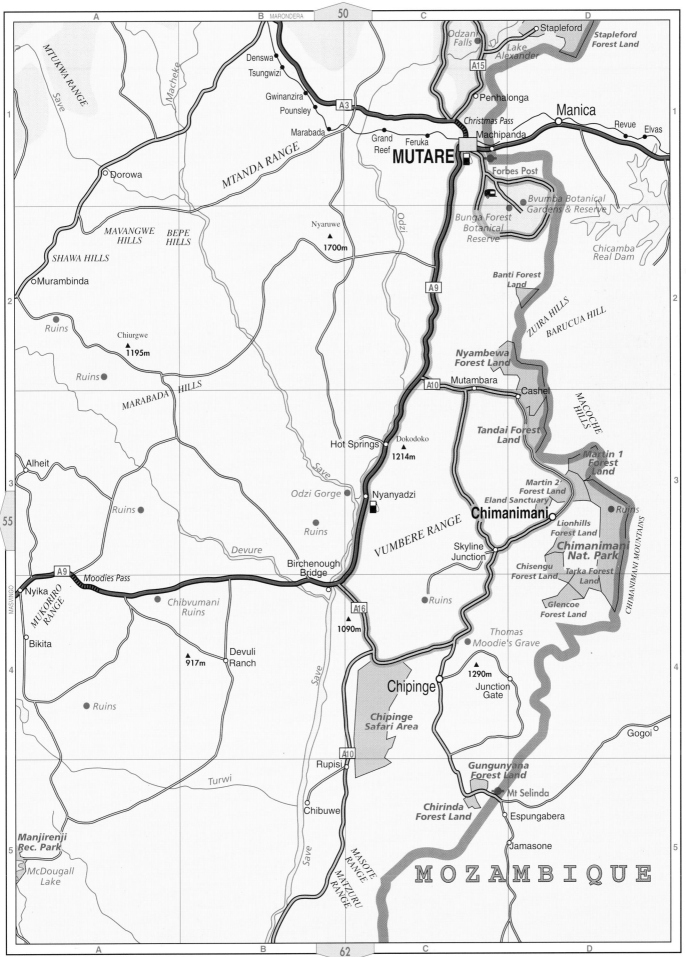

MTUKWA RANGE

Save

Macheke

MARONDERA

Denswa
Tsungwizi
Gwinanzira
Pounsley
Marabada

MTANDA RANGE

A3

Dorowa

Odzani Falls
Stapleford
Stapleford Forest Land

Lake Alexander

A15

Penhalonga

Manica

Revue
Elvas

Machipanda

Christmas Pass

Grand Reef
Feruka
MUTARE

Forbes Post

MAVANGWE HILLS
BEPE HILLS

SHAWA HILLS

Bvumba Botanical Gardens & Reserve

Bunga Forest Botanical Reserve

Chicamba Real Dam

Murambinda

Nyaruwe
▲ 1700m

Odzi

A9

Banti Forest Land

ZUIRA HILLS

BARUCUA HILL

Ruins

Chiurgwe
▲ 1195m

Nyambewa Forest Land

Ruins

MARABADA HILLS

Mutambara
A10
Cashel

MACOCHE HILLS

Tandai Forest Land

Martin 1 Forest Land

Alheit

Ruins

Hot Springs

Dokodoko
▲ 1214m

Save

Martin 2 Forest Land
Eland Sanctuary

Ruins

CHIMANIMANI MOUNTAINS

55

Ruins

Odzi Gorge

Nyanyadzi

Chimanimani

Lionhills Forest Land

Ruins

Ruins

Devure

VUMBERE RANGE

Skyline Junction

Chisengu Forest Land

Chimanimani Nat. Park

Tarka Forest Land

MASVINGO

A9
Moodies Pass

Nyika

MUKORIRO RANGE

Birchenough Bridge

Ruins

Glencoe Forest Land

Chibvumani Ruins

A16
▲ 1090m

Thomas Moodie's Grave

Bikita

▲ 917m
Devuli Ranch

Save

Chipinge

▲ 1290m
Junction Gate

Gogoi

Ruins

Chipinge Safari Area

Turwi

A10
Rupisi

Gungunyana Forest Land

Mt Selinda

Espungabera

Chibuwe

Chirinda Forest Land

Jamasone

Manjirenji Rec. Park

McDougall Lake

Save

MASOTE RANGE
MATZURU RANGE

M O Z A M B I Q U E

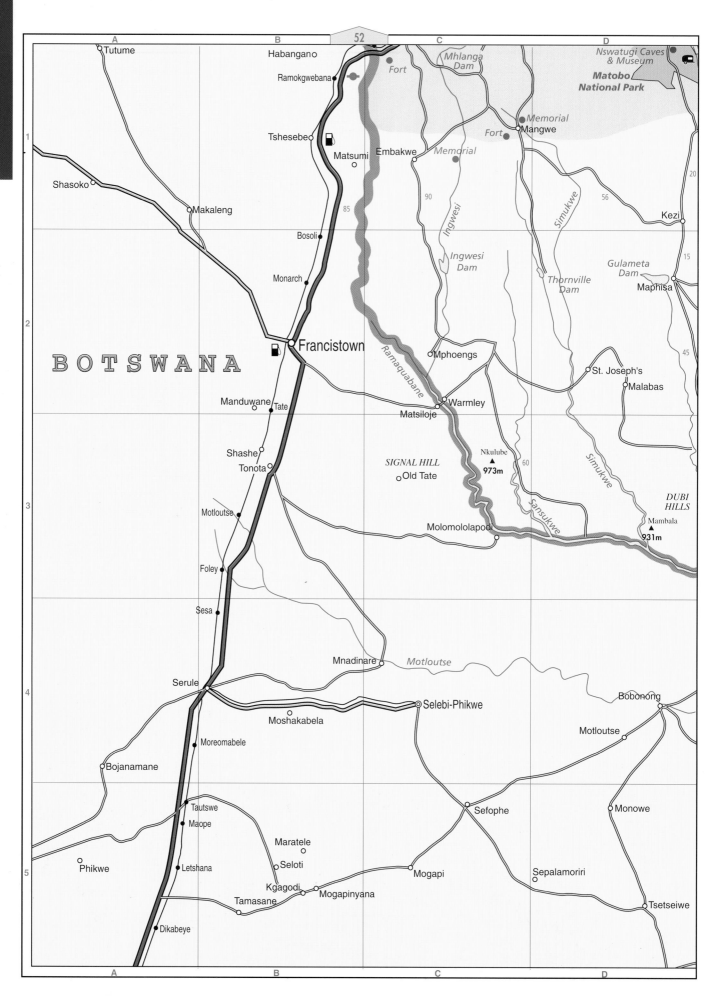

Tutume

Habangano

Ramokgwebana

Fort

Mhlanga Dam

Nswatugi Caves & Museum

Matobo National Park

Tshesebe

Matsumi

Embakwe

Memorial

Fort

Memorial

Mangwe

Shasoko

Makaleng

85

90

Ingwesi

20

Kezi

Bosoli

Ingwesi Dam

Simukwe

56

15

Monarch

Thornville Dam

Gulameta Dam

Maphisa

2

B O T S W A N A

Francistown

Ramaquabane

Mphoengs

St. Joseph's

Malabas

45

Manduwane

Tate

Warmley

Matsiloje

Shashe

Tonota

SIGNAL HILL

Old Tate

Nkulube
▲
973m

60

Simukwe

DUBI HILLS

3

Motloutse

Molomololapodi

Sansukwe

Mambala
▲
931m

Foley

Sesa

Mnadinare

Motloutse

Serule

Selebi-Phikwe

Bobonong

4

Moshakabela

Moreomabele

Motloutse

Bojanamane

Tautswe

Sefophe

Monowe

Maope

Phikwe

Maratele

Seloti

Letshana

Mogapi

Sepalamoriri

Kgagodi

Tamasane

Mogapinyana

Tsetseiwe

5

Dikabeye

Main Map Section

Matobo National Park

Silozwane Cave

Irisvale
Swazi
Sinkukwe
A6
Glass Block
Stanmore

53

Filabusi

1541m
Wanezi

Insiza

DORO RANGE

Vanguard Mine

1637m

Mwenezi

Lumane

Lomalota
1212m

Silalabuhwa Dam

Chegato

Mbauru
1060m

Malzana
1134m

25
Sabiwa
Gwanda

Antenior   Eagle Vulture   Colleen Bawn

10

Jessie

Masase

MWEZA RANGE

West Nicholson

35

Ruins   Ruins
UMCHABELO RANGE
MOSWA HILLS

Gobateme

Mchela Cave

Mtshibizini

15

Thuli

105

60

Bubiana

Ripple Creek Dam

SIKAMATSE HILLS

Kafusi

Kubungwe
869m

Mt. Towla

Legion Mine

Shashani

Kafusi Dam

Mashaba
937m

30

Mzingwane

Makado

Towla

A6

60

Kwaluzi

Hwali

730m

Zezani

Mazunga

Tongwe

Kobojango

Semolala

Machachuta   Masole

Old Fort Tuli
Pioneer Memorial
Tuli
Tuli Safari Area

643m

Giraffe Petroglyph

Tongwe Dam

BOTSWANA

Pepe

Shashe

50

Lutumba

Chamunangao

Molalatau

Motloutse

Shashe

Limpopo

Beitbridge

Mathathane   Oerwoud

Nyundo

SOUTH AFRICA

Messina

Kamkusi

N1

Baines Drift

Skelmwater

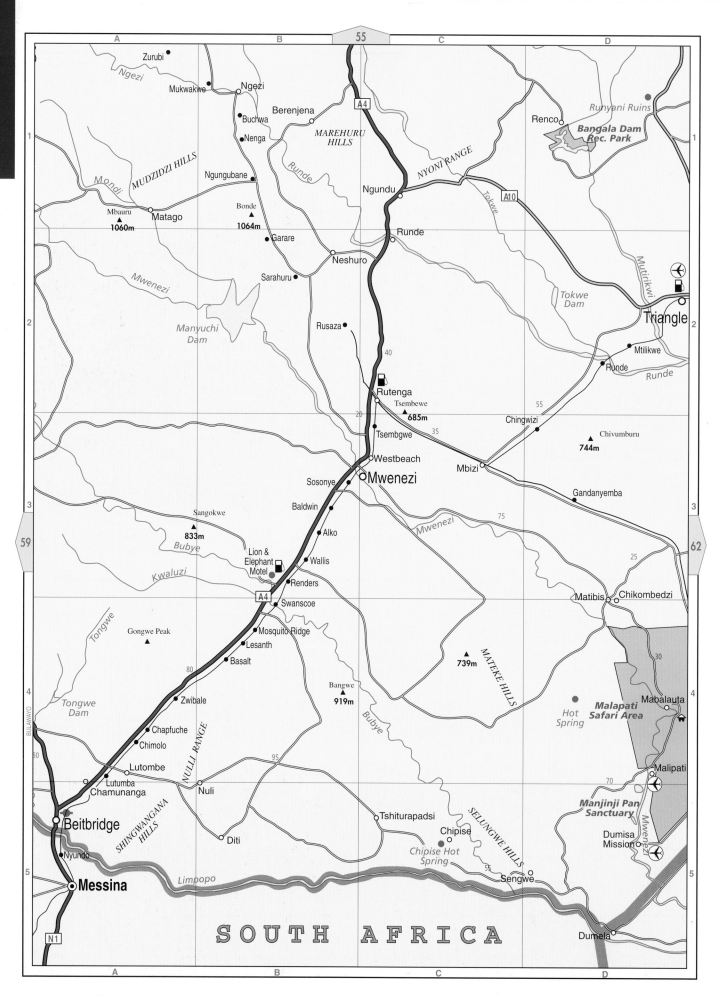

The Lowveld

Zimbabwe's southeastern segment is a harsh, hot, low-lying, monotonously flat region cut through by the Save and Runde rivers. Most of the lowveld plain is barely productive, its leached soils and sparse, sun-scorched grasses sustaining scattered herds of rangy cattle and hardy village communities that have learnt to live with drought. However, parts of it – around Triangle and the charming little centre of Chiredzi – have been irrigated and the now lush-looking land yields splendid crops. Farther to the southeast is the 5000km² (1930 sq mile) Gonarezhou National Park (see page 34).

The Lowveld and the southern parts of the Gonarezhou are served by a number of untarred roads which branch off Zimbabwe's main north-south highway, the A4, connecting Beitbridge and Harare.

The northern section of the Gonarezhou and the Chipinda Pools area is accessible via the A10 which links the Lowveld towns of Triangle and Chiredzi to the northwest.

Chiredzi Founded in the 1950s, after feasibility studies proved the agricultural potential of the lowveld, Chiredzi is the gateway to the 160km² (62 sq mile) Hippo Valley sugar cane plantations.

It is an attractive place, well served by shops, banks, clubs and, restaurants. Drawcards include the ostrich ranch and crocodile farm situated to the east of the town on the road to Birchenough Bridge.

Gonarezhou National Park

Specific points of interest within and around the Gonarezhou National Park (see page 34) include the Chipinda Pools, the dramatic Chilojo cliffs on the south bank of the Runde River, and the Tamboharta Pan, near the Save-Runde confluence, which in the wet season covers much of the ground between the Runde and Save rivers to create a paradise for bird-watchers.

There is also the Chivirira Falls, a series of 10m (33ft) cascades on the Save River, the dramatic Samahena Gorge, and the Mwatombo Pool.

Private lodges Outside Gonarezhou's boundaries, but offering easy access to the park, is the 30,000ha (74,130 acre) Lone Star Ranch. Said to be one of the largest private game reserves in Zimbabwe, it enjoys its own prolific wildlife of elephant, rhino, buffalo, lion, leopard and a host of antelope.

The ranch's Induna Safari Lodge has an informally tranquil setting, beside a dam and its rocky surrounds. It has a strikingly unusual character: weathered rock, thorn trees, thatch, window nets and open sky have all been incorporated into the design of the chalets.

The Mahenye Lodge with its magnificent riverine forest is situated at the confluence of the Save and Runde rivers on the eastern border of Gonarezhou National Park.

Above: *The Lowveld is baobab country. The larger specimens of these strangely shaped 'upside-down' trees – those with girths of 8m (26ft) and more – are thought to be more than 3000 years old.*
Below left: *Game-viewing on the giant Lone Star Ranch near Gonarezhou.*
Below: *The attractive Induna Safari Lodge, near the Gonarezhou National Park.*

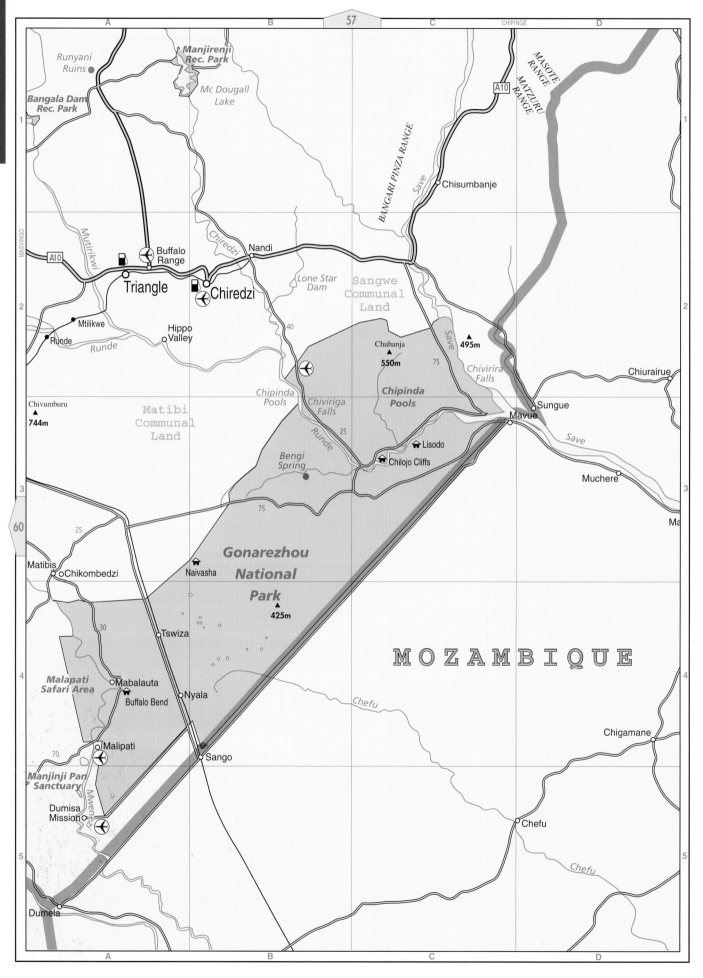

CHIPINGE

MASOTE RANGE

MATZURU RANGE

A10

Runyani Ruins

Manjirenji Rec. Park

Mc Dougall Lake

Bangala Dam Rec. Park

BANGARI PINZA RANGE

Save

Chisumbanje

MASVINGO

Muttirikwi

A10

Buffalo Range

Nandi

Chiredzi

Triangle

Chiredzi

Lone Star Dam

Sangwe Communal Land

Mtilikwe

Runde

Hippo Valley

Runde

40

Chuhanja
550m

Save

495m

75

Chivirira Falls

Chiurairue

Chivumburu
744m

Matibi Communal Land

Chipinda Pools

Chiviriga Falls

Chipinda Pools

Sungue
Mavue

Save

25

Runde

Lisodo

Chilojo Cliffs

Muchere

Bengi Spring

75

Ma

60

25

Matibis
Chikombedzi

30

Gonarezhou National Park

Naivasha

425m

Tswiza

M O Z A M B I Q U E

Malapati Safari Area

Mabalauta

Buffalo Bend

Nyala

Chefu

Chigamane

70

Malipati

Sango

Manjinji Pan Sanctuary

Mwenezi

Dumisa Mission

Chefu

Dumela

Chefu

Index

Index